# Bible Dynamics

By

Jeffrey H. Herbert

Bible Dynamics



Library of Congress Control Number: 2013916829
ISBN 978-0-9723185-2-5

First Printing March 2014

To order books, tapes, or for ministry engagements
Contact the author by mail or phone:

Covenant Life Church
P.O. Box 1262
Springfield, VA 22151
703-280-0341
Website: www.covenant-life-church.org

Bible Dynamics

www.propheticlifeministries.org

Printed in the U.S.A. by
Morris Publishing; 3212 East Highway 30
Kearney, NE 68847
1-800-650-7888

# Dedication

This book is dedicated to our Lord and Savior, Jesus Christ, who called me to the prophetic. Because of His manifold grace, He anointed me to preach and teach His Word, and to demonstrate the power of God.

# Table of Contents

# Acknowledgements

I am grateful to the Lord Jesus Christ for birthing me into the prophetic-apostolic anointing and ordaining me through Christian International, Founder, Bishop Dr. Bill Hamon and Dr. Evelyn Hamon. Thanks Bishop and Mom for your prayers, support, and love.

Special thanks to Apostles Leon and Donna Walters for all of your Fathering, mentoring, and love. May the Lord bless you for your faithful love and support that has been so vital to the continuance of our ministry.

Finally, special thanks to my wife - Linda - for your help with editing this book and praying me through to completion. Special thanks also to our friends, covenant partners and members of Covenant Life Church who continually pray for us. We are thankful for your prayers, love, and encouragement.

# Introduction

This book is written with the purpose of making Bible study more meaningful, spiritually refreshing, and life giving. The word 'dynamics' means "a change producing force."[1] When studied on a consistent basis, this is what the Bible should accomplish – a change in your life! The Word of God (the Bible) is alive with life- changing power.

I invite you to look up the scriptures as I am presenting them throughout this book and take time to meditate on them for further revelation. (After all, this book is about Bible Study!)

**"For the word of God is living and powerful, and sharper than any two-edged sword, piercing even to the division of soul and spirit, and of joints and marrow, and is a discerner of the thoughts and intents of the heart."(Hebrews 4:12)**

Over the years, I observed that many believers do not always make time to read or study the Bible. But, in these last days, we need to be believers who take time for God and His Word. There are many who claim to be Christians, but I believe there are those who are the true followers of Jesus Christ whom I term, "the Remnant believers." These are the followers who are truly sold out for Jesus! [2] One characteristic of the Remnant believer is someone who loves and knows the Word of God.

We should all be Remnant believers! But this is difficult to do unless we have an understanding of the Bible and how to apply it to our lives. I am convinced that in these last days only those who know how to believe and stand on God's Word are going to be able to survive the things that are coming on the earth. Whether the church does or does not go through the great tribulation is open to debate! But, what is not debatable is that we will all go through tribulations and trials of life. However, with Jesus Christ we have the victory through His Word – the Bible. Consequently, it is important that all believers study the Bible and make it the top priority in their life.

The Bible says in Isaiah 60:1-2,

**"Arise, shine; for your light has come! And the glory of the Lord is risen upon you. For behold, the darkness shall cover the earth, And deep darkness the people; But the Lord will arise over you, And His glory will be seen upon you."**

This verse gives us the contrast between two groups of people and their spiritual condition. For the lost, their lives will get darker and darker. For the believer, their lives will get brighter and brighter. Notice in this scripture that the world system is going to get darker or more evil in its methods. This means that life will become more challenging for everybody. But for those who trust in the Lord, God will supply the strategies and power to overcome and live in victory.

This book has been written in seven parts:

Part I: explains what the Bible is;
Part II: explains the purpose of the Bible;
Part III: explains why and how to study the Bible;
Part IV: explains how we obtained the Bible;
Part V: explains how to interpret the Bible;
Part VI: presents study methods & types; and

Part VII: presents information on advanced studies.

I believe that every part of this book has a practical application for practical living. Deep theological studies have their place, but my hope is that this book provides something for every believer, at every level of Bible knowledge and experience. And, as a disclaimer, every reader should note that this book is the express opinion of myself and does not reflect on any individual person, church, organization, or affiliation. I pray that you will be blessed as you read this book.

# Part I: What is the Bible?

## Chapter 1: The Word of God

The Bible consists of 66 different books, composed by many different writers. Writers represented almost every social rank from statesmen to peasants, kings, herdsmen, fishermen, priests, tax-gatherers, tentmakers, Jews, and Gentiles! Most of them were unknown to each other and wrote during various periods of history – over a period of 1600 years. And yet, the Bible is only one book, dealing with only one basic subject: the subject of man's redemption and the revelation of Jesus Christ.

The Bible is the inspired Word of God and has many names. Some of the most common names to identify the Bible include the Bible, the Word, the Word of God, the Scriptures and Holy Scriptures. There are other terms such as the 'Sword,' but many believers use one of the other names. The Bible is also more than just a book: it is the actual spoken Word of God. The very words are 'God breathed,' and they are inspired words. The scripture states,

**"All scripture is given by inspiration of God, and is profitable for doctrine, for reproof, for correction, for instruction in righteousness…" (2 Timothy 3:16).**

The word inspiration indicates that God inspired the very words that are written – both Old and New Testament. The following is a definition of the Greek word for inspiration: "communication which has been inspired by God."[3] Note that it does not say, dictated by God. Why? Because the Holy Spirit inspired the authors. The authors were not in some type of trance or out-of-body experience. They still maintained their personality and ways of expression. The words were not dictated - the author was allowed to use his own vocabulary and style of writing. For example, the letters written by the Apostle Paul under the inspiration of the Holy Spirit sounded like the Apostle Paul when he spoke to others. Likewise, Luke sounded like Luke! The Holy Spirit worked in such a way to communicate His Word infallibly through fallible men. Thus, every verse is divinely inspired by the Holy Spirit.

Inspiration also means that the Holy Spirit moved on the author's heart and thinking process so they wrote exactly what God wanted.[4] The authors used their own vocabulary and style of writing, and they understood what they were saying. They may not have known the proper interpretation or how it would be fulfilled, but the authors did understand the words they were writing.

Inspiration ensures us that the Word is infallible. Infallible means, "not capable of being wrong or making mistakes."[5] Because they were writing under the inspiration of the Holy Spirit, the writing was infallible. They were all equally inspired, and the writing was all infallible. The inspiration of the authors did not change their character. They retained all their individual peculiarities as thinkers or authors.

The Bible is not just any book. It is not a science book, a history book, a story book, or just a collection of writings for religious inspiration- although the Bible does contain all of these subjects! When the Bible discusses these subjects, we know that it is truth and it is accurate because it was inspired by the Holy Spirit (it is infallible).

When compared to science on some subjects, science has been found inaccurate! For example, scientists revised the theory of evolution because science itself found things that were incorrect! Yet, the Word of God has not changed its explanation of the origin of life even once in 6000 years!

In Genesis 1:1 it says,

**"In the beginning God created the Heaven and the earth."**

And, this scripture has not been disproven yet!

Another example is the debate involving Galileo. An astronomer by the name of Galileo was persecuted for saying the sun was the center of the universe and not the earth. But the scriptures make no such statement about either the sun or the earth being the center of the universe. The medieval church taught that the earth was the center, but the Bible never makes this claim. As it turns out - both the church and Galileo were wrong!

Another example is the subject of life on other planets. Some who do not believe in the Bible look to find life on other planets because they suppose it will prove the Bible wrong. But, the truth is - even if extraterrestrial life is found - it does not prove that the Bible is wrong! The Bible does not say that life does not exist elsewhere! In fact, it is not mentioned. Regardless of the subject however, the Bible addresses each topic without error.

# Chapter 2:
# The Only True Word

How do we know our Bible is the one and only true Word of God?

First, the Word of God states it is the true word. It also states that holy men were moved by the Holy Spirit to write the scriptures. No other book makes this claim for itself.

"...**Knowing this first, that no prophecy of scripture is of any private interpretation, for prophecy never came by the will of man, but holy men of God spoke as they were moved by the Holy Spirit." (2 Peter 1:20-21)**

**"For whatever things were written before were written for our learning, that we through the patience and comfort of the scriptures might have hope." (Romans 15:4)**

Second, the Old Testament was endorsed by the Lord Jesus Christ Himself.

**"These are the words which I spoke to you while I was still with you, that all things must be fulfilled which were written in the Law of Moses and the Prophets and the Psalms**

**concerning Me. And He opened their understanding, that they might comprehend the scriptures." (Luke 24:44)**

**"Then He closed the book, and gave it back to the attendant and sat down. And the eyes of all who were in the synagogue were fixed on Him. And He began to say to them, "Today this scripture is fulfilled in your hearing." (Luke 4:20-21)**

The Lord taught that Moses and the prophets wrote scripture under the inspiration of God. In fact, the Old Testament that you are reading is an English translation of the very scriptures Jesus read and taught.

**"Ought not the Christ to have suffered these things and to enter into His glory? And beginning at Moses and all the Prophets, He expounded to them in all the scriptures the things concerning Himself." (Luke 24:26-27)**

Third, the Lord indicated that there was more truth yet to be revealed at a later time. Thus, He implied that the New Testament would be written.

**"I still have many things to say to you, but you cannot bear them now. However, when He, the Spirit of truth, has**

**come, He will guide you into all truth; for He will not speak on His own authority, but whatever He hears He will speak; and He will tell you things to come." (John 16:12-13)**

Fourth, our Bible has written prophecy of which we have historical facts that prove the prophesy was accurate! Over 22 prophecies were fulfilled in the last three days while Jesus was on earth. And, these prophesy were prophesied hundreds of years before they were fulfilled.

**"For these things were done that the scripture should be fulfilled, Not one of His bones shall be broken. And again another scripture says, "They shall look on Him whom they pierced." (John 19:36-37)**

It is also noteworthy that some of the scripture was very detailed and it was fulfilled by those who didn't even realize what they were doing! See John 19:23-24.

**"Then the soldiers, when they had crucified Jesus, took His garments and made four parts, to each soldier a part, and also the tunic. Now the tunic was without seam, woven from the top in one piece. They said therefore among themselves, Let us not tear it, but cast lots for it, whose it shall be, that the scripture might be fulfilled which says: They divided My**

**garments among them, And for My clothing they cast lots. Therefore the soldiers did these things."(John 19:23-24)**

Another example is an Old Testament prophecy that was fulfilled in Old Testament times. This prophecy was fulfilled four hundred years later, and Isaiah even named the king that would proclaim it!

**"Who says of Cyrus, He is My shepherd, And he shall perform all My pleasure, Saying to Jerusalem, You shall be built, And to the temple, Your foundation shall be laid." (Isaiah 44:28)**

Below is another example of prophecy that was fulfilled in every detail:

**"Thus says Cyrus king of Persia: All the kingdoms of the earth the Lord God of heaven has given me. And He has commanded me to build Him a house at Jerusalem which is in Judah. Who is among you of all His people? May the Lord his God be with him, and let him go up!"(2 Chronicles 36:23)**

Fifth, archeologist's (experts who study ancient cultures and artifacts) and historians have confirmed many details noted in the scriptures. As previously noted, some of these prophecies are now literal historical facts.

# Chapter 3:
# Languages of the Bible

The Bible was originally written in two languages - the Old Testament was written in Hebrew, and the New Testament was written in Konia Greek. Konia Greek was the Greek spoken by the average person in New Testament times. Classical Greek was used by scholars. Greek in those times was much the same as English is now – a common universal language. Just as English is a second language in many parts of the world today, Konia Greek was a second language in New Testament times. This historical nuance would indicate that the New Testament was meant to be read and understood by the common people, and not just scholars. Consequently, from my perspective, the concept promoted by some churches that only scholars or their ministers can read and interpret the Bible is not accurate. If scholars were the only ones to understand the Bible, then the Holy Spirit would have used scholarly language and He would not encourage everyone to read His Word.

I believe God wants all mankind to read the Bible and study it! Thus, we recommend being cautious of people and organizations that discourage you from the reading the Bible. The Bible is our only source of infallible truth! I encourage you to have a noble mind and check the Word for yourself. It builds faith and protects you from deception.

**"Now these were more noble-minded than those in Thessalonica, for they received the word with great eagerness, examining the scriptures daily to see whether these things were so." (Acts 17:11) [New American Standard Bible (NASB)]**

# Part II: Purpose of the Bible

Overall, the Bible is about Jesus Christ, our Savior. In totality, the scriptures testify of Him. It reveals His birth, death, resurrection, and the plan for salvation through His shed blood.

**"You search the scriptures, for in them you think you have eternal life; and these are they which testify of Me." (John 5:39)**

## Salvation through Jesus Christ

The first and most important purpose of the Bible is to reveal the person of Jesus Christ - the Son of God - as the Savior of the world. The Bible reveals Jesus Christ, the salvation that is obtained through His Name, and the plan of redemption by His dying on the cross and shedding His blood for us to have eternal life.

The scriptures declare that Jesus Christ is the one and only Son of God. He was born of the Virgin Mary, crucified for our sins, descended into hell, and rose again on the third day. He ascended into heaven and is now sitting at the right hand of the Father God making intercession for us.

The scriptures declare that there is only way to get to heaven and that is by repenting of our sins, and accepting Jesus Christ as our Lord and Savior. We do this by saying a simple, heart-felt prayer such as the following:

**Lord Jesus Christ, Come into my heart and forgive me of my sins. I want to live for you from this moment on. In Jesus Name, Amen.**

## Other Purposes

Second, the scriptures reveal that God is a Holy God, comprising the trinity of the Father, Son, and Holy Ghost. It also reveals His purpose for creation.

Third, the Bible reveals God's character, His standard of holiness, and His great love for us. The Bible is the Living Word of God that gives us the revelation of what is right and wrong. The Word also supplies strength to the spirit man within, to resist sin.

**"How can a young man cleanse his way? By taking heed according to your word." (Psalms 119:9)**

Fourth, the Word of God is a book of principles that when followed, lead to a successful and satisfying life. Note that it does not mean a trouble-free life, but a satisfying life!

**"This Book of the Law shall not depart from your mouth, but you shall meditate in it day and night that you may observe to do according to all that is written in it. For then you will make your way prosperous, and then you will have good success." (Joshua 1:8)**

Fifth, the Word of God is the source for faith and hope when going through the trials and tribulations of life.

**"So then faith comes by hearing, and hearing by the word of God." (Romans 10:17)**

**"For whatever things were written before were written for our learning, that we through the patience and comfort of the scriptures might have hope." (Romans 15:4)**

Sixth, the Bible reveals things yet to come and assures us that evil will not prevail.

Seventh, the Bible discloses what happens to us after we die and where we will be eternally. It tells us that there is a heaven, and a hell.

# Bible Dynamics

What an awesome blessing that God gave to us when He gave us the Bible! It is a gift from God and it is all for us! This is what sets the Bible apart from all other books. None can compare with this awesome gift from God. The Bible states, man shall not live by bread alone, but by every word that proceeds out of the mouth of God (Matthew 4:4).

## Our Daily Bread

The Bible is our daily bread. It nourishes our spiritual man and is helpful and instructive for the complete Christian life. The Old Testament points to Jesus Christ coming to Earth, and the New Testament reveals His death, burial, and resurrection. The epistles of the Bible explain what the resurrection means and how it is working in our everyday life as our daily bread. The conscience is a natural guide that we all have and therefore everyone is accountable to God. But conscience can be blinded and perverted. Therefore, we need the Bible as our daily bread to guide us into all righteousness.

**"For when Gentiles, who do not have the law, by nature do the things in the law, these, although not having the law, are a law to themselves, who show the work of the law written in their hearts, their conscience also bearing witness, and between themselves their thoughts accusing or else excusing them) in the day when God will judge the secrets of men by Jesus Christ, according to my gospel." (Romans 2:14-16)**

The Bible provides instruction to guide our conduct. God gave us the Bible as a lamp to our feet to guide our path (Psalms 119:105).

**"Thy word *is* a lamp unto my feet, and a light unto my path." (Psalms 119:105)**

Jesus taught that the Word of God, as our true daily bread, is more necessary than natural food. It brings life, revelation and strength to our spirits. It is also the only foundation and resource for faith. Consequently, a successful spiritual life is impossible without the Word of God.

**"The thief does not come except to steal, and to kill, and to destroy. I have come that they may have life, and that they may have it more abundantly." (John 10:10)**

**So then faith comes by hearing, and hearing by the word of God." (Romans 10:17)**

The scriptures are filled with God's wisdom and answer the basic questions of man. They answer questions such as, "Where did I come from?" And, "What happens after I die?" The scriptures also give us revelation whether we are a simple country farmer or a Greek philosopher. The end result is that the Bible conveys the truth that God wants His people to know and to communicate to the world. Consequently, the primary purpose of the Bible is to lead people to a personal relationship with Jesus Christ as Savior. And, as our daily bread, it brings nourishment to our spirit man to live righteously in the present age.

Bible Dynamics

**"All scripture is given by inspiration of God, and is profitable for doctrine, for reproof, for correction, for instruction in righteousness, that the man of God may be complete, thoroughly equipped for every good work." (2 Timothy 3:16-17)**

# Part III: Why and How to Study the Bible

## Chapter 1: Why Study the Bible?

The Bible gives us courage to face our realities, knowledge to overcome, comfort for our mourning, and instruction to live in a Godly manner. Most major religions and cults in the world today all have a book they call scripture or the Bible. So how did we get our Bible and how do we know it is the right one? Knowing how the Bible came into existence and how we know it is the right one will build your faith and confidence in the Word. It will also give you the ability to explain to others why you believe it. The Bible contains the inspired Word of God, so a working knowledge of what it is and how it came about is important for everyone who is a Christian believer.

I believe that how we choose to spend our free time has eternal consequences. Although everyone has family and work related responsibilities, we are in charge of our free time. And, everyone can make time to devote to God's Word – if they really choose to do so! Those who do will find that God produces time for them. If you are too busy for God's Word, then you are just too busy and I recommend you alter your schedule!

Below is an example of how the devil likes to keep us so busy that we do not have time for God and His Word.

## Are You Too Busy?

"Satan called a worldwide convention of demons. In his opening address he said, we can't keep Christians from going to church. We can't keep them from reading their Bibles and knowing the truth. We can't even keep them from forming an intimate relationship with their Savior. Once they gain that connection with Jesus, our power over them is broken. So let them go to their churches; let them have their covered dish dinners, BUT steal their time, so they don't have time to develop a relationship with Jesus Christ. This is what I want you to do, said the devil, distract them from gaining hold of their Savior and maintaining that vital connection throughout their day! How shall we do this,"? his demons shouted. Keep them busy in the non-essentials of life and invent innumerable schemes to occupy their minds, he answered. Tempt them to spend, spend, spend, and borrow, borrow, borrow. Over-stimulate their minds so that they cannot hear that still, small voice. Entice them to play the radio or CD player whenever they drive. Have them keep the TV, VCR, CDs, and their PCs going constantly in their home. See to it that every store and restaurant in the world plays non-Biblical music constantly. This will jam their minds and break that union with Christ. Fill the coffee tables with magazines and newspapers. Pound their minds with the news 24 hours a day. Invade their driving moments with billboards. Keep skinny, beautiful models on the magazines and TV so their husbands will believe that outward beauty is what's important, and they'll become dissatisfied with their wives. Keep the wives too tired to love their husbands at night. Give them headaches, too! If they don't give their husbands the love they need, they will begin to look elsewhere. That will fragment their families quickly!" Even in their recreation, let them be excessive. Have them return from their recreation exhausted. Keep them too busy to go out in nature and reflect on God's creation. Send them to amusement parks, sporting events, plays, concerts, and movies instead. Keep them busy, busy, and busy. When they meet for spiritual fellowship, involve them in gossip and small talk so that they leave with troubled consciences. Crowd their lives with so many good causes they have no time to seek power from Jesus. Soon they will be working in their own strength, sacrificing their health and family for the good of the cause. It will work, it will work! It was quite a plan! The demons went eagerly to their assignments causing Christians everywhere to get busier and more rushed, going here and there. They will have little time for their God or their families and no time to tell others about the power of Jesus to change lives."[6]

So, has the devil been successful in his schemes? If you want the fullness of God in your life and you want blessing, than it is relationship with the Lord that brings this manifestation. The presence of God will not happen automatically in your life. Salvation is free, but everything else in the Spirit is pursued by grace through faith.

The strategy to attract the Lord's presence is pursuit. For example, when the blind man cried out, Jesus stopped (Matthew 20:30). If the woman with the issue of blood had not pressed in, she would not have received her healing (Mark 5:25). We must pursue God!

Your life can change regardless of your present situation or past failures. Many times our personal circumstances are created by our own decisions and passions. Obtaining the fulfillment of your destiny requires you to make your own decisions in walking out your salvation. Correct your way of thinking and your perspective of God by pursuing Him in prayer, and through His Word, and this will bring positive change to your life.

It is hard to have faith in somebody you don't know, so you need to know Jesus! This is what the Word of God will do for you – it will help you have a better relationship with Jesus. So, be willing to change and make new discoveries. Pursuing God requires motivating ourselves to pursue the Holy Spirit, and the Word of God. It requires that we overcome doubt, fear and busyness. But, the reward for being in God's presence is beyond compare.

And in the time of trouble, the Lord is our only refuge.

**"And David was greatly distressed; for the people spoke of stoning him, because the soul of all the people was grieved, every man for his sons and for his daughters: but David encouraged himself in the Lord His God." [I Samuel 30:6, King James Version (KJV)]**

# Chapter 2: How to Study the Bible

To help in understanding how to study the Word of God, it is important to consider some important points:

First, the Holy Spirit is the author of the Word. Because the Holy Spirit is the author of the Bible, I believe His presence is essential for any meaningful study. If Bible study seems dry or boring, I suggest asking the Holy Spirit to make it more real and exciting for you personally! Spending more time with the Lord in His presence is one way to make it come alive. The Holy Spirit breathes life into the Word. He makes it come alive and helps us to understand the scriptures in a way that will help strengthen us and apply it to our lives.

Second, the Bible is a love letter from our Heavenly Father, but it requires preparation to properly study it. Reading the Bible is not supposed to be a hard task, but when it is time to study it, there is a certain amount of prayerful preparation that is useful. Before you begin to study, I recommend that you pray that the Lord will reveal His Word to you. Below is a recommended prayer to stir yourself up to study the Bible:

**"That the God of our Lord Jesus Christ, the Father of glory, may give to you the spirit of wisdom and revelation in**

**the knowledge of Him, the eyes of your understanding being enlightened; that you may know what is the hope of His calling, what are the riches of the glory of His inheritance in the saints, and what is the exceeding greatness of His power toward us who believe, according to the working of His mighty power which He worked in Christ when He raised Him from the dead and seated Him at His right hand in the heavenly places, far above all principality and power and might and dominion, and every name that is named, not only in this age but also in that which is to come." (Ephesians 1:17-21)**

Third, knowledge, revelation, and wisdom are needed for proper Bible study. In this previous passage, notice that Ephesians 1:17 is a prayer for knowledge. Ephesians 1:18 is a prayer for revelation, and the remainder of the verses tells us those things that we obtain from God as we study. James 1: 5 also states,

**"If any of you lacks wisdom, let him ask of God, who gives to all liberally and without reproach, and it will be given to him."**

Consequently, we recommend that all believers study by faith, and believe for knowledge, revelation and wisdom.

Fourth, ask the Holy Spirit to reveal His Word to you as you study. It is the Holy Spirit that is going to reveal the Word and help us remember the scriptures. Revelation is the key to understanding God's Word.

**"However, when He, the Spirit of truth, has come, He will guide you into all truth; for He will not speak on His own authority, but whatever He hears He will speak; and He will tell you things to come." (John 16:13)**

It is revelation from the Holy Spirit that makes the Word come alive personally for the believer. There is nothing that compares to receiving a revelation from the Word by the Holy Spirit. It doesn't always happen every time you study, but it will happen enough that it will change your whole approach to studying the Word of God. Of course, the more we study, the more often these things happen. It also helps sharpen our discernment of spiritual things and makes hearing that 'still small voice' much easier. Additionally, there are changes that occur in our spirits that take place when we study the Word. We may not be consciously aware of it, but it does occur. This is what the scripture means when it states:

**"Being confident of this very thing, that He who has begun a good work in you will complete it until the day of Jesus Christ…" (Phil 1:6)**

There is also a difference between natural knowledge and revelation. For example, read Luke 5:4-11 regarding the miracle catch of fish. Peter was a professional fisherman whose trade was fishing. He fished on the Lake of Gennesaret all his life. He knew how to fish, and was well trained in his trade having natural knowledge of fishing. He knew when and where to fish, and he understood about water and weather conditions; yet he could not find the fish!

But Jesus had a revelation! He told Peter to launch out into the deep water and cast his nets. Now, reflect on this for a moment – here is this Rabbi carpenter telling this experienced fisherman where and how to catch the fish! Neither a Rabbi nor a carpenter would normally know much about fishing. Peter knew not to fish in the middle of the day because the fish can see the net! Consequently, experienced fishermen do not fish at night! They also do not fish in the deep part of the water because most of the fish are in shallow water where the bait is located. So, everything that Jesus told Peter to do did not make any sense to a seasoned fisherman like Peter! However, Peter was willing to try and take risk to implement the instruction Jesus gave to him. And, look what happened! Peter had knowledge, but Jesus had revelation. Revelation makes all the difference in solving a problem. And revelation is not just about problem solving. Sometimes it is a deeper understanding of scripture. Sometimes God just wants to share with you what is on His heart and mind.

So, studying the Bible can increase your knowledge, but we still need revelation. There is a lot of useful knowledge in the Word that is good and important. Note that Peter also needed knowledge of fishing to receive the miracle from the revelation of Jesus! He had to know how to navigate and row a boat. He had to know how to cast and retrieve a net. He had to know how to clean fish. But all of that knowledge didn't achieve results the night before. It took a revelation! Jesus had a revelation of where the fish were located in the lake. And because Peter obediently heeded the instruction of the revelation, a miracle catch of fish occurred. Thus, we need both knowledge and revelation for the power of God's Word to come alive, to become real and a part of our lives. Knowledge of the Word is where it all begins, but revelation makes it applicable to our lives.

Fifth, ensure your motive is pure. Motive is a very important aspect of Bible study. If our motive is to impress people or correct everything and everyone - we are not going to receive much revelation. However if our motivation is to know God and His ways so we can serve Him better – then this will bring dramatic results. Some believers know many scriptures, but they rarely get results? Why not? It may be because their motives are not pure. It is better to read one chapter and get something from it than read 10 chapters and get nothing! I recommend keeping your motives pure and you will get results.

# Part IV: How Did We Obtain the Bible?

In a previous section of this book, I addressed the topics of inspiration, infallibility and languages of the scriptures. We should now have an appreciation for how God communicated His Word to us in a way that He wanted His Word to be received. The Holy Spirit gave us what God wanted us to know. The Bible may not answer every question we have, but it does contain everything we need to know about Jesus and living a righteous life. The scriptures declare:

**"The secret things belong to the Lord our God, but those things which are revealed belong to us and to our children forever, that we may do all the words of this law." (Deuteronomy 29:29)**

**"All scripture is given by inspiration of God, and is profitable for doctrine, for reproof, for correction, for instruction in righteousness, that the man of God may be complete, thoroughly equipped for every good work." (2 Timothy 3:16-17)**

Note in the above passage that the 'man of God' referenced in this scripture is everyone - not just ministers!

We now turn to two other subjects that will give us a more complete understanding of how we acquired our Bible: manuscripts and translation.

# Chapter 1: Manuscripts

## History

Archeologists have unearthed manuscripts found in large cities around libraries and centers of education, such as Athens.[7] From these excavations and historical accounts, we learn many things regarding the ability of people to read and the ancient manuscripts. For example, we learned that many people either could not read or were limited in the ability to read. The necessity to read was not as crucial in ancient times as it is today. Many people were either slaves or indentured servants. Men who were free learned a trade from their father – just like Jesus learned from his earthly father. Young ladies stayed home with their mother until they were of age to marry. The Jewish culture was different in one respect, however, they taught their children to read what we now call the Old Testament.

In the ancient world, writing was more difficult because the mass production of paper and ink was not readily available. Writing still occurred, but it was not as prolific as it is today.

One reason was due to expense. Manuscripts were expensive due to the process of making paper. In the ancient world, paper was called ‘papyrus’ and it was a common writing material.[8] To prepare the writing product, the outer covering of the stem of the Papaya plant was removed and the inner fibers were cut into thin strips. Some of these were placed vertically, and superimposed upon them were soaked fibers that were laid horizontally. These two layers were stuck together with an adhesive substance, pressure applied, and the strips dried. The result was a yellowish piece of papyrus paper.[9]

Although the papyri were written in several languages, the majority was produced in Greek. They were produced during the period near the time when the New Testament was written, and they are extremely valuable for New Testament study. They show (as a result of studies in historical grammar) that the New Testament was written during the first Christian century, instead of later, as critics often have asserted.[10] They also help to give clarity to the meanings of New Testament words not previously well understood. The biblical papyri, dating from the second century and following, underscore the fact that the Greek text we had all along has been remarkably preserved in transmission. There is incredibly little difference between these early texts and those from later centuries, and not one doctrine is affected in the variations of the manuscripts.

## Creating Manuscripts

Some manuscripts were written on animal skins called 'parchment.'[11] In Second Timothy 4:13, the scripture states,

**"Bring the cloak that I left with Carpus at Troas when you come — and the books, (scrolls) especially the parchments."**

These type of manuscripts were remarkably well persevered because they were not subject to corrosive elements. However, this type of material was not used very often because it was time consuming and expensive. Lamb was an animal used for this and the skin was cut in thin stripes and dried.[12] Only one side was then used as a writing surface.

There were two types of ink used in ancient times: inexpensive and expensive.[13] The inexpensive ink was used for daily activities. The inexpensive ink was easily erased with just a wet cloth, resulting in the same material used repeatedly. A more expensive ink was used for important documents such as royal decrees, business records and religious writings. But both inks were created with the same fluids. The inexpensive ink of the ancients was composed of powdered charcoal, lampblack, or soot mixed with gum and water. It was intensely black and would retain its color for a long time. The more expensive ink had more gum adhesive in the mixture, and it was dark and very resilient to wear and tear.[14]

# Chapter 2: Copying the Old Testament

Copying the Old Testament was a very involved work and it was important for accurate interpretation. Recall from the New Testament that some of the disputes Jesus had with the Pharisees and the Scribes was over interpretation. The dispute was not about the accuracy of the scriptures. Similarly today, many disagreements in the church are concerning doctrine, and are not about the accuracy of the scriptures.

The work of copying the scriptures was carried out by a group called scribes. The scribes were members of a learned class in ancient Israel through New Testament times who studied the scriptures and served as copyists, editors, and teachers. [15] Scribes not only copied the documents, but they interpreted and taught them.

The scribes and all the Jews had a deep reverence for the scriptures and made exhaustive efforts to make sure copies were true to the one they copied. They would copy one word at a time, and count each word in the original from the top to the middle of the page. They then counted from the bottom to the middle.[16] Then they repeated the same process with the copy just created. If the numbers did not match, the copy was destroyed and the copying effort was started again. The counting was done by a different scribe then the one that made the copy. After this, one scribe would take the copy and compare it word for word while another scribe read the original out loud. This was to ensure that every word in the original was accurately copied into the page.

When more than one page was needed for copies of the Old and New Testament, the pages were sewn together and rolled around two spindles. This was called a scroll.[17] The writing was applied in columns usually on just one side. The pages could then be rolled back and forth. When a scroll became too aged to use it was buried in a secret location, unless it fall into the hands of the unbelievers and become defiled.

Copies were guarded by putting them into clay pots and stored in a vault. The chief scribe would keep the key on his shoulder. This key was rather large so as not to become lost. This method also identified who the chief scribe was in that particular school or synagogue. It was his responsibility to keep track of all the scrolls and also to insure that the copying scribes were accurate in their work. The copies were put back in the vault at sunset every day. They were counted to make sure every copy was returned. This procedure helped to ensure a high level of accuracy and quality.[18]

So, what did God do to ensure we have His Word? When the Jews were conquered and deported, they took the scriptures in clay jars with them. This explains why copies of the Old Testament are found all over the Mediterranean world.

The Dead Sea Scrolls are an example of this preservation. These scrolls were the greatest archeological find of the 20th century. Archeologists found many scrolls in caves in an area called Qumran, located in the area that is present day Jordan.[19] When the writing in these scrolls was compared to the Bible today, an amazing degree of accuracy was confirmed. For example, the book of Habakkuk in the Old Testament that we are reading in English today has only four words that are different from what the Jews were reading in Hebrew- 2,300 years ago! And two of those words are just a matter of spelling differences! That's incredible! And, these scrolls were written 200 years before Christ! Consequently, the unearthing of the Dead Sea Scrolls silenced some critics that claimed prophecies concerning Christ's coming were added after the event!

They also found clay tablets in the Qumran Caves. Clay tablets were used to transmit temporary messages.[20] For example, a message to a boat builder that described the change in boat dimensions would be transmitted on a clay tablet. A piece of flattened clay would be written on with a stylus and then harden with fire. When the message was received and completed, the tablet was thrown away. Military orders to field commanders were also transmitted this way. Clay tablets were not used for writing any part of the scriptures; however, this method is referred to in the Bible. Habakkuk 2:2 says,

Bible Dynamics

**“Then the Lord answered me and said: "Write the vision and make it plain on tablets, that he may run who reads it.”**

# Chapter 3: Copying the New Testament

When considering the New Testament, the same method of copying the scriptures was followed. During the first 200 years of the church, many Christians were Jews. Some of them were Jewish scribes who also served as professional copyists. The same diligent care of copying occurred with the New Testament documents, especially with the words and actions of Christ.

The gentile Christians learned from their Jewish brothers how to produce and care for documents. Some gentiles were commercial scribes that were already familiar with the art of copying documents. Paul even encouraged the creation of copies of his letters. This was to ensure that the pure doctrine of the New Testament was spread and preserved. Note the scripture below:

**"Now when this epistle is read among you, see that it is read also in the church of the Laodiceans, and that you likewise read the epistle from Laodicea." (Colossians 4:16)**

**"I charge you by the Lord that this epistle be read to all the holy brethren." (1 Thessalonians 5:27)**

The inference from this scripture is that the scriptures were copied so that all the 'holy brethren' could read it. The epistle to the Laodiceans that is referenced in the above scripture may be the

New Testament book of Ephesians which was written about the same time and sent to the same general geographical area.

# Chapter 4: Reliability of the Bible

There are two issues regarding reliability of the Bible that we will address: autographs and duplicate documents.

The first issue concerns the perspective that original writings called 'autographs' do not exist. Autographs are the exact piece of manuscript that the original author wrote on.[21] Consider for example, that today we do not have the original manuscript of the book of Ephesians, and we do not have the original writings of the other apostles. So, how do we know if we have reliable copies of the original scriptures? The answer is the same way we know we have reliable copies of the Constitution of the United States!

In Washington, D.C. there is a building called the Archives. Inside the Archives, the original copy of the U.S. Constitution is preserved in an air tight case. It is the actual document that Thomas Jefferson wrote. However, if somehow this original document was destroyed, there are copies available that replicate the original writing.

This same method applies to copies of the New Testament. The New Testament is one of the most well documented and authenticated writings of all ancient literature. It is authenticated by over 2,000 documents, some of which are fragments and some are complete copies.[22] Even though we may not have the original autographs or scrolls, we have copies of the original writing that replicate the Bible with accuracy and confidence. And, some of these ancient documents are the second or third copy from the original, dating all the way back to the second century AD.

The second issue concerning reliability of the Bible is the concern that New Testament documents are not exactly alike. The documents are very close, but there are some cases where words are added, or words are missing. Despite this, it should be noted that no one is disputing the doctrine of the New Testament, just that the documents are not exactly the same. But just like the example above concerning preserving the authenticity of the Constitution, this problem is resolved in the same way. By making a comparison between manuscripts, the words of the original are determined. The tendency of scribes was to add words, not delete them. Because of the reverence that scribes had for the Word of God, they made notes on the side of the copy they were writing in order to check the wording in another document.[23] Sometimes notes were copied into the main manuscript from the side note. For example, Romans 8:1 states,

**"There is therefore now no condemnation to them which are in Christ Jesus, who walk not after the flesh, but after the Spirit." (Romans 8:1) (KJV)**

Compare this version with the New American Standard Version of the same verse.

**"Therefore there is now no condemnation for those who are in Christ Jesus." (Romans 8:1) (NASB)**

Note how the words of the last phrase-***who walk not after the flesh, but after the Spirit***-disappear. This is because a scribe put that phrase in a side note from verse 8:4. After many copies, the note was accidentally copied into the original. But, all modern translations have this phrase removed for the following three reasons: 1) none of the early church fathers who quoted this verse in their writings included this phrase-which is an indication that it was not in the manuscripts they were using; 2) it is contrary to the doctrine of salvation by faith and not works – which is a doctrine that Paul and the New Testament writers were adamantly teaching; and 3) none of the early manuscripts that have been discovered since the King James translation was completed have these words in them.

Another example is 1 John 5:5:

**"Who is he that overcometh the world, but he that believeth that Jesus is the Son of God? This is he that came by water and blood, even Jesus Christ; not by water only, but by water and blood. And it is the Spirit that beareth witness, because the Spirit is truth. For there are three that bear record**

**in heaven, the Father, the Word, and the Holy Ghost: and these three are one." (KJV)**

Compare that with the New American Standard – Updated version (NASB),

**"Who is the one who overcomes the world, but he who believes that Jesus is the Son of God? 6 This is the One who came by water and blood, Jesus Christ; not with the water only, but with the water and with the blood. It is the Spirit who testifies, because the Spirit is the truth. 7 For there are three that testify: 8 the Spirit and the water and the blood; and the three are in agreement." (1 John 5:5) (NASB)**

Please take note of how the seventh verse, "**For there are three that bear record in heaven, the Father, the Word, and the Holy Ghost: and these three are one,**" is not quoted in modern translations. This is because during the debates of the third and fourth century when they discussed the doctrine of the Trinity, this passage was never cited, even though it is a strong reference in favor of the Trinity. This is also a serious indication that this passage was not in the manuscripts at that time when it would have so conclusively settled the issue. The ancient manuscripts were consulted and it was discovered that this passage only occurs in two very late documents.[24] So this verse is not included because it lacks manuscript support and historical verification. (It is important to note that the teaching on the Trinity does not depend on the authenticity of this verse. There are many other passages that reveal the truth about the Trinity; however, the Trinity is not a part of the scope of this book.) From these two examples however, we can see the thorough process that ensures us of the exactness of the Word. The process is also the same for both the Old and New Testament.

What did Jesus teach concerning the reliability of the scriptures?

**"For assuredly, I say to you, till heaven and earth pass away, one jot or one tittle will by no means pass from the law till all is fulfilled." (Matthew 5:18)**

So Jesus seemed to believe that the Old Testament was infallible and eternal.

**"Jesus answered them, Is it not written in your law, 'I said, "You are gods"'? If He called them gods, to whom the word of God came (and the scripture cannot be broken), do you say of Him whom the Father sanctified and sent into the world, 'You are blaspheming,' because I said, 'I am the Son of God'? If I do not do the works of My Father, do not believe**

**Me; but if I do, though you do not believe Me, believe the works that you may know and believe that the Father is in Me, and I in Him." (John 10:34-38)**

Jesus guaranteed the truth and the fact that His Father's word would be unbreakable. He staked His claim to divinity on it, and He implied that there was more truth to come after His departure.

**"I still have many things to say to you, but you cannot bear them now. However, when He, the Spirit of truth, has come, He will guide you into all truth; for He will not speak on His own authority, but whatever He hears He will speak; and He will tell you things to come." (John 16:12-13)**

What did the apostle Peter teach concerning the scriptures?

**"Since you have purified your souls in obeying the truth through the Spirit in sincere love of the brethren, love one another fervently with a pure heart, having been born again, not of corruptible seed but incorruptible, through the word of God which lives and abides forever, because All flesh is as grass, And all the glory of man as the flower of the grass. The grass withers, and its flower falls away, but the word of the**

**Lord endures forever. Now this is the word which by the gospel was preached to you." (1 Peter 1:22-25)**

**"Knowing this first, that no prophecy of scripture is of any private interpretation, for prophecy never came by the will of man, but holy men of God spoke as they were moved by the Holy Spirit" (2 Peter 1:20-21)**

What did the apostle Paul say concerning the scriptures?

"**Holding fast the faithful word as he has been taught that he may be able, by sound doctrine, both to exhort and convict those who contradict." (Titus 1:9)**

**All scripture is given by inspiration of God, and is profitable for doctrine, for reproof, for correction, for instruction in righteousness, that the man of God may be complete, thoroughly equipped for every good work." (2 Timothy 3:16-17)**

# Chapter 5: Selection of the Books in the Bible

## Why were the Books Selected?

Why were some books of the Bible chosen for inclusion in the scriptures while others were rejected? This is an important question to answer because some claim the church corrupted the original manuscripts so they could teach what they wanted taught! However, I believe this mindset was introduced to discredit the Bible.

That said, I believe archeology and other sciences prove that the scriptures are accurate! For example, the Bible refers to a group of people called the Hittite. For years there was not any evidence that such a group existed. However, a people called the Hittites were mentioned in the writings in caves along the Turkish border.[25] Another example of archeology proving the scriptures is the finding of the Dead Sea Scrolls. Previously some critics implied that there were errors in the transmission of the scriptures and some accused the church of outright fabrication. But, archeologists' unearthing of the Dead Sea Scrolls discredited this claim. Entire books of the Old Testament were found to be accurate, and they were written over 200 years before Christ. Therefore, the church could not have fabricated anything because it did not exist yet! And, when checked against the present books of the Old Testament, the accuracy is astounding! Consequently, science has proven the accuracy of the scriptures.

Personally, I believe that some people try to discredit the Bible because evil hates the truth of God's Word.

**"He who believes in Him is not condemned; but he who does not believe is condemned already, because he has not believed in the name of the only begotten Son of God. And this is the condemnation, that the light has come into the world, and men loved darkness rather than light, because their deeds were evil. For everyone practicing evil hates the light and does not come to the light, lest his deeds should be exposed. But he who does the truth comes to the light, that his deeds may be clearly seen, that they have been done in God." (John 3:18-21)**

## How Were the Books Selected?

The books as we know them today are called the Canon.[26] They were chosen by the early church councils and put into the order we now have in our Bible. The early church councils consisted of men who knew the scriptures. Some of them were taught by the original apostles. But, as the apostles and living witnesses began to die, their oral traditions were committed to writing.

**"After that He was seen by over five hundred brethren at once, of whom the greater part remain to the present, but some have fallen asleep." (1 Corinthians 15:6)**

These writings were collected as a testimony to the life of Jesus and the original apostles. Luke specifically tells us that he consulted with known eye witnesses and oral traditions (Luke 1:1-4). He then wrote the Book of Luke and Acts (under the inspiration of the Holy Spirit) - which was all one scroll when it was originally written.

**"Inasmuch as many have taken in hand to set in order a narrative of those things which have been fulfilled among us, just as those who from the beginning were eyewitnesses and ministers of the word delivered them to us, it seemed good to**

**me also, having had perfect understanding of all things from the very first, to write to you an orderly account, most excellent Theophilus, that you may know the certainty of those things in which you were instructed." (Luke 1:1-4)**

**"The former account I made, O Theophilus, of all that Jesus began both to do and teach, until the day in which He was taken up, after He through the Holy Spirit had given commandments to the apostles whom He had chosen, to whom He also presented Himself alive after His suffering by many infallible proofs, being seen by them during forty days and speaking of the things pertaining to the kingdom of God." (Acts 1:1-3)**

Luke always used infallible historical proofs. His writings would have been denied right from the beginning if they were not true. And, do not forget the promise of the Holy Spirit that the Spirit Himself would teach and witness to the things about Jesus.

Over the course of time, writings had to be evaluated to determine which were true and which were false. This became particularly critical when the book of Revelation appeared. Christians were questioning whether it was of God or not. Some philosophers were even writing things that denied the truth – thing such as denying the Deity of Jesus Christ. (All false religions and cults deny this truth.) The Old Testament was a settled matter because it was received from the Jews directly. The Old Testament consisted of scriptures the Lord Himself used, so there wasn't any question about them. The Old Testament is the very scriptures He was referring to when He said,

**"If He called them gods, to whom the word of God came (and the scripture cannot be broken), do you say of Him whom the Father sanctified and sent into the world, 'You are blaspheming,' because I said, 'I am the Son of God'?"(John 10:35-36)**

Consequently, the debate regarding the truth of the scriptures was over which books should be installed in the New Testament. This was a very serious issue - one that would determine the moral standards and truth that Christians would live by. Consequently, it took over 400 years and several church councils before the books of the New Testament were established. This is what is called the Canon of scripture, and we've had them for over 2,000 years. The Canon is the sacred Bible or collection of books, accepted by the Christian church as uniquely inspired by God. It is authoritative, providing guidelines for belief and behavior for all Christians.

It was the early church councils who determined the Canon. We are sure that the early church fathers took their work seriously. They were aware of Proverbs 30:6 which says,

**"Do not add to His words, Lest He rebuke you, and you be found a liar."**

And Deuteronomy 4:2 which states,

**"You shall not add to the word which I command you, nor take from it, that you may keep the commandments of the Lord your God which I command you. Your eyes have seen what the Lord did at Baal Peor; for the Lord your God has destroyed from among you all the men who followed Baal of Peor. But you who held fast to the Lord your God are alive today, every one of you."**

Also note that at this time in history there was only the Christian church. The Catholic, Orthodox, and Protestant denominations that we know today did not exist. So the arguments that we see today among the various denominations were not part of this process. There may have been some debate, but the goal was to arrive at the truth that all could believe. Denominational divisions were not an issue in those days. The question of who decided what books would be included in the New Testament was solely answered by the early church councils.[27]

## What Standard Was Used for the Canon?

The word 'canon' means a set rule or standard common to a group.[28] There were four main rules used as standards. The first rule was that the book must be written by one of the original apostles or an associate closely linked to them. For example, Mark was a close associate of Peter and Luke who ministered with the Apostle Paul. The second rule was that nothing in the book could contradict known historical facts or anything written in other books already accepted. The third rule was the book was known and used by the vast majority of the church. The fourth rule was called the rule of the Spirit: the writing must conform to the deity of the Lord. [29] It must be consistent with His teaching, and holiness and must witness in the spirit of the believer when it was read or heard.

[Note that I believe this fourth rule was problematic. Why? Because what one person receives as inspirational, another might not! But, I believe that what is false and what is true is easy to discover if you really want to know the truth. God made truth available and he wants you to have it more than you do! Jesus died and rose again for you to have a Living Book (the Bible) of absolute, infallible truth. Hebrews 4:12 states: "For the word of God is living and powerful, and sharper than any two-edged sword, piercing even to the division of soul and spirit, and of joints and marrow, and is a discerner of the thoughts and intents of the heart."

That is the beauty of our scriptures. They can be translated into anyone's language and they are understandable, life giving and have brought truth to many people, tribes, and generations year after year for hundreds of years. No other book can change life like the Bible, because no other book is of God and invested with His Spirit and power. This is what sets the Bible apart from all other books in the world.

Compare this to something like the 'lost books of the Bible.' The lost books have accounts of Jesus that do not bring truth. For example, one account is of Jesus cursing a small boy who then dies from the curse! Another story is of Jesus expanding Himself till He became 25 feet tall! I believe that these stories of Jesus are not true. But, the Bible is true and it states, "Heaven and earth will pass away, but My words will by no means pass away." (Matthew 24:35)

I believe that some unsaved people fabricate reasons to discredit the Bible. Why? Because their heart and conscience tell them they are not right with God. So they want reasons to deny Godly truth so they can continue in their sinful life style. I also believe that some who participate in false religions may have prideful religious spirits. They say, "I am special because only I know the real truth." It is this pride, along with their own efforts to be righteous, that appeals to them and this blinds them to the truth of God's Word. Second Corinthians 4:4 states: "Whose minds the god of this age has blinded, who do not believe, lest the light of the gospel of the glory of Christ, who is the image of God, should shine on them."]

Books that complied with these four rules were accepted into the Canon. The four gospels and Acts were accepted, as well as most of Paul's writings. Books that had a more difficult time of being added included Philemon, Hebrews, James, First and Second Peter, Jude, and Revelation. Philemon, First and Second Peter and Jude were questioned because of rule three - it had to be a book known to and used by the vast majority of the church. Because these books were so short in composition, they did not have as wide a distribution among churches as did the others. Therefore, after much debate they were received into the Canon because of the high degree of inspiration and conformity with the other three rules. James was discussed by the councils at length because it seemed to contradict Paul's writings about salvation by faith violating rule two (James 2:14-26). Also, there was a question about authorship. But overall if the scriptures complied with the rules, they were accepted.

During evaluation of the scriptures, however there were other problems that arose. One problem was the authorship of books. For example, there are three people in the New Testament that are named James. So, which one wrote the book of James in the New Testament? It was decided by the church councils after much study and debate. In this example, the council determined the author was the Apostle James – Jesus half-brother. One of the ways they determined this included the doctrine of salvation. The book of James indicates that true saving faith should produce good works because if someone did not have good works their faith was a dead faith. Apparently, the early church fathers were of the same opinion because in the second century it was received as an inspired book of the official Canon.

The last two books - Hebrews and Revelation – experienced the greatest amount of debate. The book of Hebrews violated rule one, which states the book had to be written by one of the original apostles or an associate closely linked to them. Consequently, many authors were proposed by council members and scholars to be the writer of the book of Hebrews. The Apostle Paul, Luke, and even Barnabas were all considered. Much of the book sounds like Paul, although the Greek style of writing was similar to Luke. To this day, no one can say with any absolute certainty who wrote Hebrews. By the late third century, Hebrews was finally accepted into the Canon for the same reasons as First and Second Peter. Hebrews addresses many revelations of Christ's glory and the superiority of the New Testament over the Old. It is clearly inspired scripture.

Revelation's main problem was a matter of interpretation. The scholars of the church council demonstrated that the symbolism in the book of Revelation generally conformed to the symbolism used in the book of Daniel. From a historical perspective, some of the prophecies of the book were beginning to come to pass during the lifetime of the council members! Some council members believed it was the only book that confirmed Christ's final victory over evil and the triumph of the church. Meanwhile, the council determined that the Apostle John wrote the book. Consequently, in the third century it was officially received along with First, Second, and Third John.

## Summary

The Bible is the inspired, infallible, written Word of God. It was written by inspired authors who used their own vocabulary to communicate the exact words God wanted to communicate. The Bible was not dictated, but the Spirit moved on different authors to convey what God wanted to be written, without error. The Word of God was transmitted in Hebrew for the Old Testament, and Greek for the New Testament. There is also a small portion of the book of Daniel that was written in Aramaic.

The accuracy of the Bible has been challenged, however archeology and science has proven the Bible to be true. Examples were given of how the Bible was challenged and how the Word was proven correct every time. This reveals that God said what He wanted to say, to free us from error.

Small errors may have occurred while copying manuscripts; however the original manuscripts were restored. They were restored by studying how the early church fathers used them and by reconfirming the manuscripts. The U.S. Constitution is an example of how an original manuscript could be destroyed and yet the content can be restored.

The New Testament is one of the most comprehensively verified documents of all ancient literature. If questionable materials were removed from the Bible, the teaching they give could be established by other scriptures, all spanning over 2,000 years. Only the hand of God could accomplish such a feat!

How did we obtain the Bible? We discussed manuscripts, ink, copies, and preservation. We examined the establishment of the Canon and how church councils determined the books that are in the current Bible. Then, we discussed the rules for canonization. In summation, we learned how God communicated His Word and how we obtained our Bible.

We are now at the end of the fourth century in this dialogue of explaining how the Bible came about. We now understand that Hebrew and Greek manuscripts were codified into one book called the Bible, and the Bible is a miracle book from a miracle- working God who loves us and died for our sins!

# Chapter 6:
# Text Type and Translations

In studying how the Bible was translated into English and other languages, text type must be considered. A text type is a collection of manuscripts usually found in one geographical area and sharing a common reading or characteristic with the manuscripts within the group.[30] Most of the differences in the words found in a translation are due to the text type of the translator.

There are three main text types, the Byzantine, Alexandrian, and the Western – named after geographical regions or cities. In the fourth century, the Roman Empire (after the time of Jesus Christ) split into two empires. In the east was the Greek-speaking Byzantine Empire whose capital was Constantinople. In the west was the remainder of the Roman Empire. The capitol was Rome and the common language was changing from Greek to Latin. Alexandria was a city in Egypt. While technically a part of Rome, the Alexandrians did what they wanted since Rome was too weak to control them.

The Byzantine text has the greatest number of Greek manuscripts. The reason for this is twofold. First, in the west, Latin was beginning to replace Greek as a common language. So, of course, fewer copies of Greek were made. The second reason was due to the influence of Islam. The Muslim invasion had conquered most of North Africa and parts of Europe, such as Spain. Obviously this significantly hindered the work of copying Christian scriptures. Therefore the Byzantine text type was dominated over all others. It was later called the Textus Receptus, or Received Text. It was the text type that the translators of the Bishops Bible and the King James Version used. No official church body ever authorized this text type exclusively, but this text has manuscripts that date back to the fourth century. The theory behind this text is that many manuscripts for comparison make for a more accurate text.

There are two basic groups of text types in use today, the Byzantine text or Authorized Text used by the King James tradition and the Nestle-Aland (NA) text.[31] The NA accepts the most ancient readings (Alexandrian) as the most accurate. There is another group that uses which ever variation appears the majority of the time in the manuscripts as the most reliable. This is designated as the Majority text designated by the letter M for Majority Text. The Nestle-Aland and Majority Texts so closely resemble each other that they are considered as one text type.

Today all modern translation except the New King James Version uses the Nestle-Aland text type because it's based on better scholarship, is closer in age to the originals, and is verified by the historical record more often. Each text type has its own strengths and weaknesses. The variations between text types only involve the spelling of Greek words, word order, and two paragraphs in the gospels. Overall, both text types agree most of the time.

It is important to understand at this point that when we discuss copyist errors, we are not saying the Bible has errors in it! The Bible is infallible and accurate. We would not even bring up this subject except for the fact that some people try to make a dispute out of the fact that different text types have different words in the scriptures in some places. As already stated, the entire issue of copyist error involves less than a page and a half of the entire New Testament and does not affect any doctrine in any way whatever! There can be a copying error in the manuscript, but the manuscript is still God inspired and infallible.

## Translations

So how did the translations shift from the Greek of the third century to the English version used today? In the very beginning, churches were located in places that are known today as Iraq and Iran, and they are still present today. These cultures neither read nor spoke Hebrew, Greek, or Latin. They read and spoke Aramaic. Therefore the Hebrew Old Testament and Greek New Testament were translated into Aramaic. This occurred after the Canon was established. It was labeled the Aramaic text, and it is used by Arab Christians today. This translation is one of the very first translations completed by the Christian church. The Aramaic was translated into English and today it is referred to as the Eastern Bible or Eastern Text. It can be found in some Christian book stores, and is amazingly close to the King James Version.

The next key translation was completed by a man named Jerome. He was one of the most eminent scholars of the early church and was asked by Pope Damascus in 383AD to update the scriptures.[32] He translated the Hebrew and Greek into Latin, which was the language of the Western church. This translation was named the Latin Vulgate. The terms of predestination, justification, supererogation (superego), sanctification, salvation, mediation, regeneration, and revelation all first appear in the Old Vulgate. From these terms grace, redemption, election, reconciliation, satisfaction, inspiration, and scripture all came about with a more clear meaning."[33]

The word "Vulgate" means "common recognized text or version."[34] It lends credence that in the fourth century the Bible was meant to be read and understood by everyday people. It wasn't until much later in the Middle Ages that the church began to forbid any translation other than its own and prohibit the people from reading it. This is because church doctrine had strayed so far away from Scriptural truth that their doctrines could not stand in the face of even a cursory glance at the Bible.

(My recommendation is to be careful of anyone, group, or church that does not want you reading the Word of God for yourself! Sometimes there is a hidden agenda that is not of God or there may be a false doctrine, revelation, or concept they want you to accept that may not be of God! It is always good to read the Word of God for yourself and know the scriptures!)

**"But there were also false prophets among the people, even as there will be false teachers among you, who will secretly bring in destructive heresies, even denying the Lord who bought them, and bring on themselves swift destruction. And many will follow their destructive ways, because of whom the way of truth will be blasphemed. By covetousness they will exploit you with deceptive words; for a long time their**

**judgment has not been idle, and their destruction does not slumber." (2 Peter 2:1-3)**

Jerome was accused of disturbing the peace of the Church and shaking the foundations of faith. But the new translation gradually came into use equally with the older version, and replaced it. Then, as now, there are those who automatically oppose any new translation. Sometimes it's because of fear. Nothing touches the heart of a believer like the topic of there being something wrong with the book they consider the Word of God. All translations should be critically reviewed for truth and correctness.

**"And you shall know the truth, and the truth shall make you free." (John 8:32)**

However, as the science of translation improves we should be able to receive the benefit of that process by keeping a teachable spirit. The Vulgate was the version used by the Western church for almost eleven centuries, while the Eastern or Orthodox Church continued with the Greek version based on the Byzantium text.

The next translation that impacted the church occurred in 1456 AD when William Tyndale completed a translation in English from the original Greek manuscripts.[35] All versions in the

West until that time where basically revisions of the Latin Vulgate. Bible translations and versions began to increase during this time. Why? First, Constantinople fell to the Muslim Turks causing the Greek scholars of the East to immigrate to the West, especially England. They brought the Byzantine text with them, and then the invention of the printing press made mass production of the Bible possible. Second, one of the most momentous and powerful developments was the Protestant Reformation. With the Church of Rome's authority and doctrine being challenged, there was a cry of return to the scriptures. Martin Luther and other reformers began to proclaim that the scriptures were the sole and final authority for faith, not the pope or church traditions. This caused a concern for the accuracy of the versions. Consequently, they went back to the Byzantine text since the Latin Vulgate was considered a Catholic Bible.[36]
The Reformers then began to translate from the Byzantine Greek text, which the vast majority of all English Versions have used up to the twentieth century. This is often referred to as the Received or Authorized text type.

During this time in history, King Henry the Eighth of England made himself the head of the Church of England. He rejected the Pope and removed the Roman Catholic Church from being the only church in England.[37] This was done more for political and personal motivations than anything religious. It was not because of any religious fervor on his part. We know from history that the king needed his divorce legitimized so he could marry another woman.[38] This was because he needed a male heir to assume his throne. But, God gets the glory even out of man's actions because later King James the First authorized a new translation in 1611 that would become what is known today as the Authorized or King James Version. King James did this in order to restrain the disputes about doctrine among his own bishops and silence the critics of the Bishops Bible - a version translated by Matthew Parker, archbishop of Canterbury, and nine other bishops.[39]

The King James Version is based on the Byzantine text due to the fact that that was the most reliable and readily available text at the time. The King James Version translators did in fact check other text types like the Aramaic. However, the Byzantium text was followed almost exclusively. The King James Version is hailed as one of the most accurate and poetic translations ever created. It has been used by millions over the last four centuries. It has impacted the lives of more English- speaking people than any other translation until recent times.

With the advancement of archeology and the discovery of manuscripts much closer to the original - a change in the text type used by translators was about to take place. Today we have text types not available to the translators of 1611 because they were not discovered yet. These text types are called the Alexandrian or

Egyptian Text. This text type reflects the scholarship of the last two centuries.

When we consider variations in text types we have to keep in mind that we are talking about less than one percent of the entire Word of God. The New Testament is one of the most heavily attested documents of all ancient literature, but even the opponents of the Bible admit the text is accurate. With some opponents the debate is whether the words are inspired. Some opponents reject the Bible as the word from God. But the Bible says,

**"Heaven and earth will pass away, but My words will by no means pass away." (Matthew 24:35)**

## King James Controversy

This brings us to controversy regarding the King James Version of the Bible. There are those who claim that the King James Version is the only true version of the Bible, and all other modern versions are in error. Some people claim there was an Alexandrian cult, who in the fourth century corrupted the Greek text that the Nestle-Aland is based upon and is now used by modern versions. They also claim this cult exists today and modern scholars are a part of this cult, and that they are trying to deceive the believers! But, there is no evidence to support these claims regarding error. And, no one can find the cult! Regardless, the "King James only people" continue to claim all other versions are in error.

So, let's investigate this claim! The King James Version was written in 1611 AD. Consequently, if the King James Version is the only true Word of God, where was the Word of God for the 1,600 years of the church? If this charge has merit, then what happened to all the believers that could not read English? Did God leave them without His Word? Further, the King James version itself has been revised five times! So, which one of the five revisions is the accurate one? So, as we ask some fundamental questions, we see that this claim does not make sense!

Consequently, it is not a question of which translation is better, but it is a question of which text type do you prefer? Let's just look at some of the differences so we can have a more complete understanding of the differences between King James Version (Byzantine or Authorized Text) and modern versions (Nestle-Aland). Consider the following scriptures:

**"In whom we have redemption <u>through his blood</u>, even the forgiveness of sins." (Colossians 1:14) (KJV)**

**"In whom we have redemption, the forgiveness of sins." (Colossians 1:14) (NASB)**

This is a good example of the divergence in text type. Notice how the words "through his blood" are not in the New American Standard version. All modern versions translate this verse without these words. Why? Because these words are not in the Nestle-Aland or the Majority Text. This is one of the prime examples the 'King James only' (people who only believe in and read the King James Version of the Bible) people point out. But again, the difference is in text type – it is not a conspiracy! The 'King James only' people make the claim that this proves that modern versions are trying to remove the blood from the Bible and it is all part of a conspiracy on the part of today's scholars. But, if this is true, then someone did a poor job of it because references to the blood of Jesus are still in all these verses: Romans 3:25; 5:9; Ephesians 1:7, and there are many more! If someone was trying to remove references to the blood of Jesus from the Bible, then why did they leave all these verses in the Bible? Here's another example:

**"This is he that came by water and blood, even Jesus Christ; not by water only, but by water and blood. And it is the Spirit that beareth witness, because the Spirit is truth. For there are three that bear record in heaven, the Father, the Word, and the Holy Ghost: and these three are one. And there are three that bear witness in earth, the spirit, and the water, and the blood: and these three agree in one." (1 John 5:6) (KJV)**

**"This is the one who came by water and blood — Jesus Christ. He did not come by water only, but by water and blood. And it is the Spirit who testifies, because the Spirit is the truth. For there are three that testify: the Spirit, the water and the blood; and the three are in agreement." (1 John 5:6) [(New International Version (NIV)]**

Notice the words that are underlined. These words disappear in the New International Version and all other modern versions. Why? Because these words only appear in two very late manuscripts, and there is not enough manuscript witness to support this verse. Also, during the trinity debate of the fourth century this verse was not quoted. This also indicates these words were not in the Bible during this time because they would have referred to them if these words were in the text. I believe these words crept into the Byzantine text from a margin note.

Let's look at two more examples: John 7:53 thru John 8:11and Mark 16:9-20. The verses John 7:53 thru 8:11 appear in the manuscript record where they presently are in our Bibles. However in some manuscripts they appear in the book of Luke. So, the issue is not whether this is authentic scripture, but rather what is its exact location in the gospel accounts? This is why some Bibles put these verses in brackets.

The ending of the book of Mark is more complicated. The book of Mark ends at verse eight, and the remainder of the verses - Mark 16: 9-20 - do not appear in two of the most ancient copies of the New Testament. Nevertheless they appear in almost all other manuscripts - over 900 of them! For this reason, they are included as scripture, but they are put in brackets. The King James Version and the New King James Version are based on the Byzantine text type. Modern translations are based on the Nestle-Aland or the Majority Text. This is what creates the differences in versions that we see in Bibles today.

So the question is, which text type do you prefer? Most believers have a version that they favor. The problem occurs when one group wants to force everyone to use its version! As long as we understand that the difference is merely in text types and has nothing to do with accuracy, we will be able to use our favorite version without any fear or concern. When someone else's translation varies slightly from yours - don't get upset! And, if you prefer the King James Version - then use it!

# Chapter 7:
# Translation Theory

A practical knowledge of Translation Theory will help you understand how all the different translations originated and the differences between them. So, what is translation and how does it function?

Translation is taking a word as it was understood by the original author and applying a word that conveys that idea to the current reader.[40] Sometimes an entire phrase has to be considered, but the purpose is to always to present to the reader what the original author intended. In order to do this, the culture and style of the author must be taken into account. For example, Paul and Luke were educated men who wrote with a different vocabulary and style than Peter and John.

**"Now when they saw the boldness of Peter and John, and perceived that they were uneducated and untrained men, they marveled. And they realized that they had been with Jesus." (Acts 4:13)**

When interpreting the translation, note that the Holy Spirit can teach truth through anyone that spends time with Jesus. It is also helpful to understand the culture and time period when the scriptures were written. Some examples are as follows:

**"If your enemy is hungry, give him bread to eat; And if he is thirsty, give him water to drink; For so you will heap coals of fire on his head, And the Lord will reward you." (Proverbs 25:21-22)**

At first, this may seem to indicate that charity should make your enemy feel ashamed. However, if you know the Hebrew custom, the verse becomes clear. On the Day of Atonement, the custom was the high priest would fill his censor with "coals of fire," and then to put incense into it resulting in a sweet-smell. If we apply this custom to this Bible passage, the Holy Spirit is saying that as we do good to someone who does not deserve it, we are burning away shame that we experienced. And then prayer, confession, and thanksgiving will rise as incense to the throne of God as a sweet smell to God. Thus, "we shall overcome evil with good."

Below is another example,

**"Judge among yourselves. Is it proper for a woman to pray to God with her head uncovered? Does not even nature itself teach you that if a man has long hair, it is a dishonor to him? But if a woman has long hair, it is a glory to her; for her hair is given to her for a covering. But if anyone seems to be**

**contentious, we have no such custom, nor do the churches of God." (1 Corinthians 11:13-16)**

This verse is referring to another custom of culture. The unmarried woman of New Testament times would wear a veil to promote proper etiquette and control passions. Although the appropriate control of sexual passion is still a New Testament doctrine, this particular custom does not apply to every church or situation today.

**"But if anyone seems to be contentious, we have no such custom, nor do the churches of God." (1 Corinthians 11:16)**

Veils on women were not required in every place even in the time of the Apostle Paul. Notice also the expression 'churches of God.' This is a strong indication that a church was not to have dominion over another church. Each local assembly was allowed to practice non-essential doctrines and customs as they deemed appropriate. The passage concerning veils merely is indicating that there should be a clear distinction between men and women! Also, proper respect should be shown to each gender. From these two examples we can see that understanding the culture helps us to understand what God is saying.

I do not believe God is mandating we live according to the cultural customs of New Testament times. But, I do believe the

Word of God is eternal, and its principals are always applicable. And, this makes the Bible a book for all ages, generations, and cultures.

# Chapter 8:
# Types of Translations

There are three methods of Bible translations: word for word, dynamic equivalent, and paraphrase. The three methods of translation all have advantages and disadvantages, but all have the same goal of producing an understandable and useful version to read. Consequently, every translation must consider two things: 1) accuracy to the original intent of the author; and 2) clarity for the sake of the reader.

The word for word method of translation functions as follows: a translator looks at the original word in the manuscript and seeks to find an exact word for it in the receptor language (in our case English) consistent with what the author was inspired by God to say. The King James, New King James and the New American Standard Bible are all examples of this method of translating that are addressed in this book. The advantage of this method is a high degree of accuracy to the original intention of the author. The disadvantage is they can be somewhat difficult to read. Keep in mind that all translations have the issue of sacrificing accuracy for clarity, and that is the reason for different methods of translation.

The dynamic equivalent translation method works in the following way: instead of translating word for word, this style translates phrase for phrase or thought for thought.[41] This allows the translator the freedom to find an exact equivalent word by using other words in the phrase. An example;

**"In this was manifested the love of God toward us, because that God sent his only begotten Son into the world, that we might live through him." (1 John 4:9) (KJV)**

**"This is how God showed his love among us: He sent his <u>one and only Son</u> into the world that we might live through him." (1 John 4:9) (NIV)**

Notice how the New International Version - a dynamic equivalent translation - changes the phrase 'begotten Son' into 'one and only Son.' This translation uses three words to replace the word 'begotten.' This is because the word begotten in English means, 'to procreate'[42] This definition infers that Jesus had a beginning, but if Jesus is God, then He cannot have a beginning! The Bible says that He is the I AM, or the one who always was alive! The word begotten comes from the Greek word <u>*monogeneses'.*</u> It means, 'single unique only one of its kind.'[43] So in this particular case the New International Version sacrificed accuracy for clarity, however it is closer to the original intent of the author. It allows us to understand clearly that the Bible does not claim Jesus had a beginning, but rather, that He always was!

(Note there are some groups that believe Jesus had a beginning, but this belief is contrary to scripture).

All translations must make these choices between accuracy and clarity. Even word for word translations sometimes have to give up some accuracy so an English reader can grasp it. For this reason, I prefer translations that use a committee of translators from various denominations and faith groups. A committee helps remove denominational bias from the translation and insures that accuracy is not being sacrificed for the sake of clarity. The problem is that when we strive to be so accurate, sometimes we cannot understand the scripture! But, when we strive to be so simple, we may lose the accurate meaning of the scripture.

Some translations remove theological words such as sanctification, justification, redemption, and many others because they claim they want to make the scripture clearer. But, this is not translating – this is paraphrasing! For example, some translations change the term 'justification' into a phrase that says, 'it is just as if I never sinned! While this might be a proper reflection of what the word means, it is difficult to teach the doctrine of justification if the word 'justification' is not in your Bible!

Some translations also change the word 'tongues' into the word 'languages' because the translators are opposed to speaking in tongues! But, by changing the term, this may bring a theological bias into the translation. The Greek word 'gloossa,' can mean 'language,' but the primary meaning is 'tongue.'[44]

The last translation method is called a paraphrase. With this style of translation the translator reads the manuscript and then uses his own words to translate the meaning. Consequently, a paraphrase is not a translation; rather it is someone's opinion!

The following are some translations that I recommend to the reader for consideration to use as your personal Bible:

- NEW KING JAMES VERSION (NKJV):

It is based on the Received Text and the text type matches the King James Version (KJV) almost word for word. It has the advantage of making the language more modern without changing the meaning. The NKJV is helpful for those who were accustomed to KJV, but want something that is easier to read and understand.

- KING JAMES VERSION (KJV):

The KJV has a poetic style and prose that can make memorization and meditation easier. It is an accurate version, however the text is the old style English.

- NEW AMERICAN STANDARD BIBLE (NASB):

This is one of the most literal word for word translations in English that is available today. It is based on the Alexandrian or Nestle-Aland text type. If the reader likes absolute word for word translation from a modern text type, then this is the version to read.

- NEW INTERNATIONAL VERSION (NIV):

This version is based on the Nestle-Aland or modern text type. It is a dynamic equivalent in terms of the style of translation. In my opinion, this is one of the best dynamic equivalents, although it sacrifices some accuracy for clarity, but not enough to cause great issue with the doctrines of the church. This version also comes in the New International Readers Version, which is a gender-neutral translation.

- NEW REVISED VERSION (NRV):

It has the same text type and translation style of the NIV and is gender-neutral.

- NEW LIVING TRANSLATION (NLT):

This is a modern text type, dynamic equivalent and is gender-neutral. This version translates all measures of time, distance, and weight into modern equivalents so it is easily understood. The NLT translation converts historic dates into modern equivalents when the date can be historically identified. For serious Bible students, this may not be the optimal version to use for doctrine, teaching, or memorization. However, it can help the reader to understand the scripture more clearly when truth has been established by a more accurate version.

- AMPLIFIED VERSION (AMP):

A version that seeks to give clarity to the Hebrew and Greek words found in the manuscripts. It does this by using brackets and parenthesis and inserting additional words in English. A parenthesis is used to indicate additional meaning of words found in the text. The brackets are used to indicate other justified English words or phrases. It also has some historical footnotes.

Of those versions mentioned above, I believe the more accurate are the New King James Version, King James Version, New American Standard Version Updated Edition, New International Version and New Revised Standard Version. However, what is important is that you read the Bible, understand it and apply it to your life! I also recommend that if you have concerns regarding the Bible version you are reading, then consult your pastor or spiritual leader and ask their opinion.

## Summary

This chapter explained what the Bible is and how we obtained it. The Bible is the inspired infallible Word of God. The scriptures reveal God's plan for man and plan of salvation. The Bible consists of two divisions called the Old and New Testaments, separated in time by an interval of nearly four hundred years. The Bible is divided into 66 sections that are called 'books:' 39 books are in the Old Testament and 27 books are in the New Testament. Twenty-two of these books are historical, five are poetical, 18 are prophetic, and 21 are written in letter form.

The scriptures contain revelation, poetry, songs, hymns, history, biography, stories, parables, law, and most importantly – they reveal God's nature. There are at least 36 different authors who wrote from three different continents, different countries, different languages, and from different occupations. Among these authors were kings, farmers, mechanics, scientific men, lawyers, generals, fishermen, ministers and priests, a tax-collector, and a doctor. Some were rich, poor, city-bred, country born, touching all the experiences of mankind and extending over 1,500 years. And yet the Bible is one cohesive book because God was the real author! Throughout time, God never changed His character or moral law, or contradicted Himself.

We obtained the Bible from manuscripts made of various materials such as papyrus and animal skins. The ink of the ancients was composed of powdered charcoal, lampblack, or soot mixed with gum and water. It was intensely black and would retain its color for a long time. The more costly ink had more gum adhesive in the mixture. It was dark and very resilient to wear and tear.

In this chapter we also addressed how the copies were carefully produced, and maintained, and we discussed the various translations. A professional class of copyists called scribes hand copied from one manuscript to another to make new manuscripts. This section addressed translations to include the history, methods, text types and concerns regarding translations.

# Part V: Interpretation of the Bible

## Chapter 1: Literature Types

God has expressed Himself in every form of literature known to man. Please recognize that the type of literature you are reading is important in order to receive the proper interpretation of a particular passage or verse of scripture. Note that, although books may be classified as certain types, they may have other types of literature within them. For example, Genesis is considered the first book of the law, but it also has history and prophecy in it.

The following is a brief synopsis of eight literature types found in the Word of God.

1. LITERAL: A literal interpretation means there is not a hidden meaning.[45] It is adhering strictly to the basic meaning of words. Although the Bible is a powerful, life-giving book, it speaks to us in every day common language. When symbolism is being used, it will be clear that it is to be understood as a symbol. Some have thought the Bible has hidden meanings and this has created confusion and deception throughout the history of the church. Be careful of those that claim there are hidden meanings

that only they can see! The symbols should be understood as we commonly use symbols. The interpretation of biblical symbols should arise naturally from a sanctified common sense, and from how they are used in other scriptures and within the context of scripture. For example:

**"For you shall go out with joy, and be led out with peace; The mountains and the hills Shall break forth into singing before you, And all the trees of the field shall clap their hands." (Isaiah 55:12)**

Clearly the Bible does not literally mean that hills are going to sing or trees are going to grow hands and clap. The symbols should be understood that even creation will rejoice when God's Word is manifest. This interpretation is confirmed by Romans 8:19, which states,

**"For the earnest expectation of the creation eagerly waits for the revealing of the sons of God."**

But, compare this scripture to the one below! The literal truth of Matthew 4:4 will impact the rest of your life!

**"But He answered and said, It is written, Man shall not live by bread alone, but by every word that proceeds from the mouth of God." (Matthew 4:4)**

2. SYMBOLISM: Symbols are used to help people understand things that have a spiritual meaning. People think in pictures, and not words, so it is an effective method of conveying a great deal of spiritual revelation in a way that can be readily understood and remembered. The key to understanding symbols is to look for the literal truth they represent. For example, in Revelation 1:16-20, the stars in His right hand are the seven angels of the seven churches. Consequently, symbols should be understood in their context, both in the current passage being studied, and the overall context of scripture. All symbols represent literal truth. The symbolic prophecies of Christ's first coming were literally historically fulfilled, and so will the prophecies of His second coming.

3. ALLEGORICAL (figurative): Allegory means, having hidden spiritual meaning that transcends the literal sense of a sacred text."[46] A perfect example of this is Galatians 4:22-26. In this scriptural passage an entire story is symbolic.

**"For it is written, that Abraham had two sons, the one by a bondmaid, the other by a freewoman. But he who was of**

**the bondwoman was born after the flesh; but he of the freewoman was by promise. Which things are an allegory: for these are the two covenants; the one from the mount Sinai, which gendereth (gives birth) to bondage, which is Agar (Hagar). For this Agar (Hagar) is mount Sinai in Arabia, and answereth (corresponds) to Jerusalem which now is, and is in bondage with her children. But Jerusalem which is above is free, which is the mother of us all." (Galatians 4:22-26) (KJV)**

In this passage the Apostle Paul uses the story of Sarah and Hagar to convey the difference between the Old and New Covenants. He tells us that the law is bondage, while grace sets us free.

In the early history of the church, Augustine emphasized allegorical and symbolic interpretations to an extreme. Everything in the scriptures meant something different from the plain understanding of the way words described. I believe that this error helped to lead the church into the Dark Ages. It removed clear biblical revelation from the church, thus making it powerless. Another sad result was wrong doctrine that began through inaccurate interpretation of the scriptures. Then, when the church proclaimed itself to be infallible, these doctrines could not be changed. But, the only infallible truth is the scriptures!

4. PROPHECY: These are predictions about the end-times; and they can also be special messages from God to a person

that is given through the Gift of Prophecy.[47] The focus of all prophetic truth is Jesus Christ, who was destined to be the greatest prophet. He declared God's truth in this age and the age to come. As the embodiment of truth, Jesus Christ fully revealed the character and love of God, which the earlier prophets reflected only partially.

5. PARABLE: A short, simple story designed to communicate a spiritual truth or a religious principle, or a figure of speech in which truth is illustrated by a comparison or example drawn from everyday experiences.[48] There is usually one basic truth that a parable is teaching. For example, the parable of the ten virgins (Matthew 25) is teaching us to be spiritually alert because we do not know when the Lord will return.

**"Afterward the other virgins came also, saying, 'Lord, Lord, open to us!' But he answered and said, Assuredly, I say to you, I do not know you. Watch therefore, for you know neither the day nor the hour in which the Son of Man is coming." (Matthew 25:11-13)**

When you are reading parables, always look for the one truth that God is trying to deliver. The primary meaning is found in the context in which the parable is given. Also, note that the Lord gave a teaching on how to understand parables in Matthew

13:1-23. There is a great lesson on the use of symbols in this passage because parables are by nature symbolic stories.

6. DOCTRINE: The New Testament epistles (letters) written by the apostles - Romans through Jude. This type of literature teaches the practical application of our salvation in Christ Jesus. In my opinion, doctrine is the most important part of the entire Bible.

7. WISDOM: The Wisdom books consist of Job through Song of Solomon. Job is a historical Hebrew poem telling the story of a real person named Job and his trials in life over many years. Psalms was written to music and sung in the temple. Proverbs is a wisdom book that teaches practical living. Ecclesiastes is contrast between worldly wisdom and spiritual revelation. Song of Solomon is the wisdom of love.

Most people could not read, so they remembered scripture through song and poetry. This kind of literature often has a deeper form of expression to encourage worship and produce wisdom. Many of the Psalms were sung among the people during the work day to remind the Israelites of the greatness and grandeur of God.

8. HISTORIC: Historic means events that actually happened in the past.[49] Throughout the books of the Bible, there are historical accounts. Some people say that the book of Genesis

is so beyond science and their common reasoning that they cannot accept it. But Jesus taught from Genesis and all the books of Moses (Genesis, Exodus, Leviticus, Deuteronomy and Joshua) as historic facts that truly happened. Some say that Jesus was just accommodating Himself to the superstition of the times. But, if this was true then that would make Him a liar!

The book of Genesis describes a culture and events that are foreign to us. But, that does not mean it did not occur. It is a mistake to think that every natural process we observe in the world today has always operated that way. For example, science discovers laws of physics being violated in the cosmos every day. Why is it so hard to understand that the same thing can happen here on earth? To ignore the creator's ability to supersede or control His own creation relegates God into the same category as the man-made gods of Greek myth, which is the place most people and scientists would like to put Him! If the Bible says something happened, then that is what happened. If the Bible says something is going to happen, you can count on it!

Under historic literature, we also need to address the purpose of genealogies. The first and most important purpose of historical accounts in the Bible is to trace the lineage of the Lord Jesus Christ. Matthews's genealogy traces Jesus lineage through Joseph, thus proving He is eligible to be called the King of Israel. Luke's genealogy traces His lineage through Mary and demonstrates that He is the Son of God.

Another purpose is to identify the peoples of the nations. God does not recognize the boundary lines on a map made by man. He deals with man and the nations as they exist, but His redemptive and prophetic purposes follow the plans He has for people groups.

**"And He has made from one blood every nation of men to dwell on all the face of the earth, and has determined their preappointed times and the boundaries of their dwellings" (Acts 17:26)**

The tenth chapter of Genesis is called the table of nations, and from it we can trace the people groups of the nations. This becomes especially important when considering prophetic scripture.

**"And will go out to deceive the nations which are in the four corners of the earth, Gog and Magog, to gather them together to battle, whose number is as the sand of the sea." (Revelation 20:8)**

We know from the genealogies that Magog is a nation north of Israel called Russia. We can also pinpoint the time of some historic events from the genealogies. However, be aware of the fact that the genealogies are not chronological, nor do they list the descendants in order. There can be large gaps of time between names. Consequently, the genealogies cannot be used for this purpose.

# Chapter 2:
# The Organization of the Bible

Today's Bible is organized according to literature type. In the Old Testament, the historic books are Genesis through Esther. Wisdom literature is located in Job through Song of Solomon. Prophecy or prophetic books are Isaiah through Malachi. The prophetic books are divided into two sections; Major Prophets (Isaiah through Daniel) and Minor Prophets (Hosea through Malachi). The difference between Major and Minor Prophets is only in the size of the books - it does not mean that one prophet or book is less inspired or more important than another. In the New Testament the historic books are Matthew through Acts. The doctrinal books are Romans through Jude. There is only one prophetic book in the New Testament, the book of Revelation.

Although the books have a primary literature type, there may be a mix of types in them and they are not arranged chronologically. For example, Ezekiel 17:1-10 is a parable in a prophetic book, and Matthew 24:1-31 is a prophecy in a historical book. And, they are not chronological. For example, the events in Job occurred long before the events in Exodus. The point is that the books are classified according to the main literary features and style of the work.

## General Guidelines

There are some general guidelines that will help the reader interpret and study the Bible: context, receive, meditate, interpret, and apply.

1. CONTEXT:

The first guideline is to read and interpret all scripture within the context of the chapter. This means that you interpret scripture according to the scriptures around it.[50] By taking a scripture out of context, or out of the chapter, you can make the Bible say anything. I recommend that you always read the scriptures above and below the scripture you studying. By using this method, you will understand the topic and meaning of the passage better. For example, Romans 11:29 states,

**"For the gifts and the calling of God are irrevocable." (Romans 11:29)**

Using just this passage, out of context, some have preached that a believer's gift and calling is never revoked. But, we know from scripture that both King Saul and Judas Iscariot had their gifts and callings removed didn't they? Judas Iscariot was hand-picked by Jesus to be an Apostle, yet his calling was revoked because of sin.

When we read the entire 11th chapter, however, we see that the topic is talking about Israel in relation to the gospel. In context, this verse is saying that all the promises that God made to Israel's forefathers are still in effect and will be fulfilled in the future. Israel has not been excluded from salvation through Jesus Christ. Any Jew who professes faith in Jesus Christ can be saved. In context, this verse has nothing to do with the ministry gifts and callings of a believer. Unfortunately, because of this wrong teaching, some believers may be waiting until a more convenient time in their life to serve God! Consequently, it is easy to see how just one wrong interpretation of the scripture can have serious consequences for a believer. That is why the scriptures say in James 3:1-2,

**"My brethren, let not many of you become teachers, knowing that we shall receive a stricter judgment."**

Remember that anyone who teaches truth is also capable of teaching error. For this reason, it is always best to search the scriptures and read them in context.

**"These were more fair-minded than those in Thessalonica, in that they received the word with all readiness, and searched the scriptures daily to find out whether these things were so." (Acts 17:11)**

Note also, that this verse says they "received the Word," but "searched the Scriptures." This is what it means to be 'fair minded.' This is also how you keep a 'teachable spirit' - being open to learning new things. A legitimate minister of the Bible is not going to object to someone checking the scriptures and then asking questions so they can learn.

Another example is Romans 8:28.

**"And we know that all things work together for good to those who love God, to those who are the called according to His purpose." (Romans 8:28)**

Now read Romans 8:26-30. What is the topic? The topic is intercessory prayer and praying in the Spirit. Again many believers like to quote half a verse, "all things work together for good," but they miss the condition of the scripture. The scripture in context is saying that as we love God and pray in the Spirit then everything will work together for my good. Why? Because we will be following God's perfect will for our life. Our life may not be perfect, but God will help us through it.

Here is another example from the Old Testament.

**"My people are destroyed for lack of knowledge. Because you have rejected knowledge, I also will reject you from being priest for Me; because you have forgotten the law of your God, I also will forget your children." (Hosea 4:6)**

Some believers quote this scripture and say that the lack of knowledge is what destroys people. But is that what this verse is saying? Notice that only half of one verse is being quoted. A complete reading of just the verse itself tells us that it is addressing priests or the ministry that has rejected the knowledge of the Lord, the Word of God. Now read Hosea 4:4-10. This makes it clear that what is being taught here is a corrupt priesthood was causing a corrupt people. No doubt a lack of biblical knowledge is the cause of a lot of natural and spiritual destruction; however that is not what this verse is teaching. This scripture is teaching that if the ministry you listen to is presenting truth from the Word of God, then the knowledge you receive will properly guide you through the issues of life.

While no minister is perfect, the ministry you follow should be exalting the Lord Jesus Christ and His Word. They should have a thorough knowledge of the Bible, God's principles, and be people of integrity.

I believe that the lack of knowledge on the part of most Christians is causing a falling away from knowing God and it can lead to people becoming involved with false teaching and cults.

Sometimes this is due to believers not properly studying the Word of God. The lack of knowledge of God's principles can lead to destruction.

**"That we should no longer be children, tossed to and fro and carried about with every wind of doctrine, by the trickery of men, in the cunning craftiness of deceitful plotting" (Ephesians 4:14)**

Below is an example of the guideline of 'context' as it pertains to culture.

**"But every woman who prays or prophesies with her head uncovered dishonors her head, for that is one and the same as if her head were shaved." (1 Corinthians 11:5)**

It is important to read this scripture within context of the culture it is given. This scripture was written by the Apostle Paul, under the inspiration of the Holy Spirit to the believers at Corinth – a city in Greece. This city was like the 'Las Vegas' of its day! All kinds of sexual immorality were practiced in Corinth. Therefore the Holy Spirit, through Paul, in order to distinguish between Christian woman and the loose women of that culture, admonished them to demonstrate their purity and submission to authority by wearing a covering on their head. This became the cultural custom for that time, under those conditions. It was not a rule for the entire church for all time.

2. RECEIVE:

The second guideline is to 'receive' or believe what you are reading. Whatever verse or passage you are studying, make a decision to believe what you are reading!

There are several methods you can use to help you receive the Word. One recommendation is to personalize the text and make what you're reading the truth for you. For example, insert your name where personal pronouns are used and then meditate on what the scripture is saying. Another method is memorizing scriptures. Select a scripture that is helpful to you. For example, when I'm anxious about something, I speak out loud from memory the following scripture:

**"Be anxious for nothing, but in everything by prayer and supplication, with thanksgiving, let your requests be made known to God; and the peace of God, which surpasses all understanding, will guard your hearts and minds through Christ Jesus." (Philippians 4:6-7)**

Then I do what the scripture says. This is the way to use the Word of God to ward off spiritual attack when it comes – speak the scripture.

3. MEDITATE:

The third guideline is to meditate on the scripture and ask yourself, who, what, where, and why. When reading the scripture ask yourself, "Who is speaking, who is he speaking to, what are they talking about, and what is the spiritual activity going on around them?" Also ask, "What events are occurring, and what are the people saying and doing?" This can help us understand what is meant by the scripture. These questions, and others like them, bring the passage into clearer understanding.

For example,

**"And so also were James and John, the sons of Zebedee, who were partners with Simon. And Jesus said to Simon, "Do not be afraid. From now on you will catch men." (Luke 5:10)**

Using the guideline above, we learn that Jesus is speaking to Peter, James, John, and those with them. They are talking about fishing - both natural and spiritual. The spiritual activity going on around them is the miraculous catch of fish that just happened. It is taking place on the shore of sea of Galilee. Now ask, "what are they saying and doing?" Answer: Peter just realized that he is a sinful man and the others were astonished at the catch of fish. Consequently, Jesus was relating natural fishing to fishing for men. The result of this miracle was that they became His disciples.

Note that not every question applies to every verse, since some scriptures only communicate information or record historic events.

4. INTERPRET:

The fourth guideline is to interpret the scripture. In this guideline, interpret means to discover the truth of what is being said in the passage, not establish a doctrine.[51] Interpretation refers to what the passage is saying to you. And, understanding the scripture within context is one of the most important points to proper interpretation.

My recommendation is to always look for connecting words to help with proper interpretation. For example, words such as: if, and, or, but, therefore, for, in order, and that, will help you discover the flow of the author's thoughts toward the subject. For example,

**"And we know that all things work together for good to those who love God, to those who are the called according to His purpose." (Romans 8:28)**

Notice the connecting word "and." This word indicates that verse 28 is connected to verses 26 and 27. Another example is Matthew 13:18.

**"Therefore hear the parable of the sower:" (Matthew 13:18)**

'Therefore' in this verse connects the thoughts in Matthew 13:17. Consequently, as you consider the connecting words in the scriptures, the interpretation becomes more accurate.

5. APPLY:

The fifth guideline is to apply what you learned from your Bible study. Ask yourself the following questions: What should I learn from this study? What should I believe? What is God like? What did He do for those in the scripture that I can believe He will do for me? What are the promises? What conditions must I meet to receive the promise? What verse should I memorize? What is the overall impression that I learned from this passage?

## Conclusion

The interpretation of scripture should be more accurate as you use the general guidelines of context, receive, meditate, interpret, and apply. However, if you are still having difficulty, ask your pastor, or check with a high-quality commentary. Also, be encouraged that the Holy Spirit will meet you at whatever level of education and experience you have obtained and He will inspire you. He is the author of our faith so He knows exactly how to teach the scriptures to us. Remember that He loves you, and He wrote the scriptures for you. So, remain open to the leading of the Holy Spirit to teach you the scriptures and simply ask Him to reveal His Word to you and He will do it!

# Part VI: Study Methods & Types

## Chapter 1: Introduction

There are various types of Bible studies that have different purposes. Which one you use is a matter of personal preference. Whatever you choose, just remember you don't have to pick one and continue with it for the rest of your life! You can change types or mix and match anytime you desire. And, studying the Bible is not supposed to be drudgery or hard work. The Holy Spirit wants you to be spiritually strengthened and renewed by it. This is not to say that every Bible study is going to be a supernatural experience each time, but it will get better each time you study.

**"As newborn babes, desire the pure milk of the word, that you may grow thereby." (1 Peter 2:2)**

Obviously, a baby doesn't mature in one day and he has to eat more than once! So it is with Bible study. We grow with time. It is my experience that when we apply what we learn we will grow in faith. We want faith to achieve practical results from what we study. This is when study becomes rewarding and fun - when we apply it and see the results. The Bible is a living book that can achieve results like no other book. For example, I cannot recall a single time when studying my Algebra book gave me peace of mind during a time of struggle! In fact, usually Algebra was the struggle! But, I do have plenty of memories of the Bible giving me peace of mind when I studied it. Consequently, I recommend studying the Bible to find help, comfort, peace, and strength.

The Bible should be studied like a miner digging for gold! Just like digging for gold, you may not find the main vein the first time you stick the shovel in the dirt. However, 'digging' in the Bible is a worthy pursuit, because the truth you learn for yourself and apply for yourself becomes reality for you.

The scriptures themselves encourage us to read and study the Bible. Although there are some today who believe accurate interpretation of the Bible can only come from church leaders, the scriptures declare scripture is not of private interpretation. The Holy Spirit wants all of us to read and study His Word.

**"Knowing this first, that no prophecy of scripture is of any private interpretation" (2 Peter 1:20)**

**"Then the brethren immediately sent Paul and Silas away by night to Berea. When they arrived, they went into the synagogue of the Jews. These were more fair-minded than those in Thessalonica, in that they received the word with all**

**readiness, and <u>searched the Scriptures daily to find out whether these things were so.</u> Therefore many of them believed, and also not a few of the Greeks, prominent women as well as men." (Acts 17:10-13)**

The scriptures themselves declare that no individual or group has all the answers. No one is the infallible interpreter of the Bible, except the Holy Spirit Himself. I recommend that when you receive teaching from someone, check the scriptures for yourself and ask the Lord for revelation on the meaning of the scripture. Anyone can be wrong. Always check the actual Word of God (the Bible) to see that the interpretation is right.

It is important also to remember that when using a study Bible, the study notes are the work of someone who could be interpreting wrongly. Every study Bible is subject to the personal ideas and bias of the author. For example, some study Bibles either ignore, or teach against, speaking in tongues. Also, some of them say that healing is not for today, or that it passed away with the last apostle. It is unfortunate that some Bibles teach these things. When a believer is searching for more of God or trying to get healed, it is more difficult to have faith to believe God for a healing when unbelief is taught in the Bible you are studying! Consequently, it is important to obtain the complete and accurate interpretation of the Bible.

# Chapter 2:
# Study Methods

There are different methods to ways to study the Bible but whatever way you choose, I recommend that you do it daily and systematically. The occasional reading of a few verses here and there is always good, but it is not a real bible study. You will not discover the deeper things of the Word by this method. Strong 'remnant' warriors build themselves up by diligent and consistent study. The Bible was not written to just give pastors a book to preach from. It was written to change our lives, renew our minds, build our faith, and reveal God's ways and character. There are some easy methods for studying the Bible that will aid you during your study. One method is to develop a way to mark the scriptures using different colors of markers for different topics. For example, use a blue marker to mark verses that refer to the Holy Spirit, use red for the blood of Jesus, and green for eternal life, etc. Also, underline a passage or verse that has great meaning for you and you will find that later these scriptures will speak to you again.

Meditating on the scriptures is another method of study. This method will reveal deeper truth as you ponder and think about the scripture. As you meditate on it, the Lord may reveal more about the scripture that is personal to encourage you. Make a small note to yourself right in your Bible as He gives you the revelation so you remember it in the future.

Keeping a journal is another method. Keep a journal with the notes and revelations that you obtain as you study the Bible. Write down your questions as you study or make note of the truth you discovered while studying the Word. Soon you will have a Bible and journal of notes that really speak to you and are personal for you! When revelation becomes personal, than Bible study becomes fun.

## Study Tools

A successful study time requires having the study tools you need to begin study. There are basic tools you should have for your Bible Study. I recommend having a notebook, pen, colored marking pencils, concordance, and a Bible that you can write notes in the margins. I also recommend using more than one translation – use your favorite and another one that is easy to read for clarity, such as the New Living Translation or New International Version. During study, if you find a word or concept that you do not understand, I recommend using an easier translation to understand the meaning rather than using detailed word study.

I recommend that you approach the Word in an attitude of faith and reverence for the author of the Bible. Ask the Holy Spirit to reveal His Word to you. You can use these scriptures as a prayer before you begin your study:

**"However, when He, the Spirit of truth, has come, He will guide you into all truth; for He will not speak on His own authority, but whatever He hears He will speak, and He will tell you things to come." (John 16:13)**

**"But the anointing which you have received from Him abides in you, and you do not need that anyone teach you; but as the same anointing teaches you concerning all things, and is**

**true, and is not a lie, and just as it has taught you, you will abide in Him." (1 John 2:27)**

# Chapter 3: Types of Bible Study

In this chapter, I will discuss different types of bible studies to include topical, book, chapter, character and devotional. The names of these types describe how they work. Please remember you are allowed to change types any time you like. However I recommend you stay with one type long enough to receive from it and then you can decide which one you like the best. The Lord will speak to you out of which ever type you pick. He wants you to enjoy your time with Him.

1. TOPICAL:

Topical Bible study means to pick out a topic and study this topic throughout the Bible. This method can help show you what God says on that topic – through the entire Bible. It will highlight all of the scriptures on a topic from the Old Testament to the New Testament. Also if you're struggling in a certain area or need scripture to pray on a certain topic, the topical Bible will help you find the answers and promises in the Bible on that topic. This method takes time, but it helps you understand God's entire Word on that topic.

There are many topical Bibles, however one recommendation is the Thompson Chain Reference Study Bible. In my opinion, this study Bible is one of the most complete study

Bibles, since all the verses of scripture are arranged topically, without interpretative comments from anyone. With this Bible, the believer can study and discover truth on their own with the added advantage of having topical references. But, whatever Bible you choose, the goal is to interpret and understand the Word correctly. The Word declares,

**"Be diligent to present yourself approved to God, a worker who does not need to be ashamed, rightly dividing the word of truth." (2 Timothy 2:15)**

'Rightly dividing' means to let everything that the Word says about a particular topic be revealed so that we receive the complete truth on that topic.[52]

Other recommendations include the Open Bible, and the Spirit Filled Life Study Bible. The Open Bible is available in the King James Version and some other modern versions. The Spirit Filled Life Study Bible is geared for the Spirit Filled believer who wants a full gospel perspective.

2. BOOK:

Book study means to study a book of the Bible.[53] To begin this method of study, I recommend picking out a short book such as Ephesians, First John, or Philippians. Read the whole book in one period of study. Then, during the next study time, go back to the first chapter of the book you are studying. Underline the important words in each verse. For example,

**"Blessed be the <u>God</u> and <u>Father</u> of our Lord Jesus Christ, who has <u>blessed us</u> with every <u>spiritual blessing</u> in the <u>heavenly places</u> in Christ, just as <u>He chose us</u> in Him before the foundation of the world, that we should be holy and without blame before Him in love, having predestined us to <u>adoption as sons</u> by Jesus Christ to Himself, according to the good pleasure of His will, to the praise of the glory of His grace, by which He made us accepted in the Beloved." (Ephesians 1:3-6)**

Use this style for each chapter of the book. When you're done, then read the entire book again in the next study session. Now, you will have the important words of that book highlighted where you can more readily see them. This style will assist you in seeing the main thrust of each verse and chapter. Next, in one study time for each chapter, make notes in your notebook for each verse. Ask yourself, "what does this verse mean?" "What is God saying to me?" "How can I apply this truth?" "Is there something I need to repent of or change?" "What have I learned from this about God's ways, thinking, and character?" "What does it reveal about how God feels about me and how He wants to relate to me?"

Please note that not every verse can be studied alone. Sometimes several verses must be in context to understand the meaning. For example, Ephesians 2:11 should include verses 12 and 13 to make sense. Also, not every question can be applied to every verse. These are just suggestions on what to focus on as you study.

3. CHAPTER:

This method is studying one chapter at a time and it works the same as the Book method in the previous section. This method works well for those that have only a short amount of time for bible study. Chapter study is one of the most effective ways to study the larger epistles or letters of the Apostle Paul, or larger books like Psalms and Deuteronomy.

4. CHARACTER:

Character study is just as the name implies - studying a person such as Jesus, Abraham, Moses, David or Peter. This method consists of selecting a person to study and then reading about their life story. One excellent charter study is Jesus. The life of Christ is a character study that can take an entire life time, but will certainly bring much revelation.

So, how do you do a character study? First, find all of the scriptures in the Bible that pertain to your selected person. Use a concordance to find the first scripture where the person's name is mentioned. Then read their life story in one setting. In the next study time, go back and mark or put in your notebook places or events that you want to investigate further. Be sure to note their victories and failures in life. Then, ask yourself these questions: "What are their victories and what caused the victory?" "What are their failures and what caused the failure?" "How did God relate to them?" "Did God reject someone for one failure?" "How did they know they heard from God?"

There are some general observations we can make concerning this method of study. First, you will learn how God speaks to His people. We can also see a little of ourselves in each character. Second, you will see that the closer your relationship is to God the more likely your success. Third, we can ask ourselves the same questions as we did in the study and learn important things about our own lives. For example, ask yourself questions such as, "Am I doing anything like they did to cause their victory or failure?" "Is there anything I need to correct?" By asking and answering these questions, we can often relate our lives to the lives of these Bible characters and correct our ways.

Note that when you study historical accounts, there can be substantial amounts of time between events. For example, the rebellion of Absalom against David took three years to complete. It was not over in a week as it seems when we read the text! So keep this in mind when you are doing character studies – note the period of time between events in their lives.

5. DEVOTIONAL:

A devotional study is study of a portion of scripture that we feel inspired to study. Usually, this is inspired by the Holy Spirit and is personal for us. The Holy Spirit wants to reveal the Word to you. He wrote it so we could have a revelation of God and His ways. He enjoys fellowship with us and there are things yet to come in your life that He wants you prepared to receive.

The word 'devotion' in Hebrew means a "demonstration of faithfulness in the context of a mutual relationship."[54] In Greek it means a "concentration on something with delight."[55] Devotion also means, "something done with consistence because of the value we give to it."[56]

**"My soul breaks with longing For Your judgments at all times." (Psalms 119:20)**

**"I have rejoiced in the way of Your testimonies, As much as in all riches. I will meditate on Your precepts, And contemplate Your ways." (Psalms 119:14-15)**

**"But He answered and said, It is written, Man shall not live by bread alone, but by every word that proceeds from the mouth of God." (Matthew 4:4)**

Devotional Bible study is different from all other types. Many times devotional Bible study involves being silent before the Lord and waiting for Him to speak. I recommend starting this method of study by worshipping the Lord first and then moving into a time of praying in the Spirit. Then pray, "Father in Jesus name speak about anything you want to say from the scriptures, for I am listening."

We can expect the Lord to speak to us because we are sons and daughters by the blood of Christ. We are adopted into the family of Jesus through his shed blood and we are joint heirs with Him. Romans 8:15 calls us sons.

**"For you did not receive the spirit of bondage again to fear, but you received the Spirit of adoption by whom we cry out, "Abba, Father." The Spirit Himself bears witness with our spirit that we are children of God, and if children, then heirs — heirs of God and joint heirs with Christ, if indeed we suffer with Him, that we may also be glorified together." (Romans 8:15-17)**

Consequently, I recommend that you always approach the Father God as a son or daughter. Anything less is below your covenant privilege. With that truth firmly established in your heart, you are now ready to hear from your Father what He wants to reveal to you through the Bible study.

It is important to note that with this type of Bible study, the rules of interpretation do not necessarily apply. Here is an example of how this applies in a devotional study. I was seeking the Lord regarding finances for my congregation. I was quietly waiting before the Lord when He said, "Go to Psalms 10." As I read and meditated on this chapter, the Lord spoke to me again and said, "Verses 2-7 refer to the investment bankers of today. There is a plot to catch the poor."

**"The wicked (bankers) in his pride persecutes the poor; Let them be caught in the plots which they have devised. (They have plots) For the wicked boasts of his heart's desire; (This is the attitude of their hearts) He blesses the greedy and renounces the Lord. The wicked in his proud countenance does not seek God; God is in none of his thoughts. His ways are always prospering; Your judgments are far above, out of his sight; As for all his enemies, he sneers at them. He has said in his heart, I shall not be moved; I shall never be in adversity." His mouth is full of cursing and deceit and oppression; Under his tongue is trouble and iniquity."[57] (Psalms 10:2-7)**

Then the Lord said, "Verses 8-10 refer to credit card companies - they lurk like a lion to catch my people in their net of debt."

**"He *(credit card companies)* sits in the lurking places of the villages; In the secret places he murders the innocent; His eyes are secretly fixed on the helpless. (i.e., The constant bombardment of credit card applications in the mail and the**

**pressure to buy). He lies in wait secretly, as a lion in his den; He lies in wait to catch the poor; He (credit card companies) catches the poor when he draws him into his net. So he crouches, he lies low, That the helpless may fall by his strength."[58] (Psalms 10:8-10)**

I believe that the Lord revealed to me that some people were being trapped into paying off more debt, due to all of the easy credit being available. And, I believe He said to warn them about having more credit card debt and using variable interest rates in home mortgages.

Consequently, I warned the people in my congregation. Some were grateful and told me their homes were later saved from foreclosure because they did not buy using variable interest rates! But notice, nothing within the context of Psalms 10 has anything to do with credit cards or bankers. Yet, this was the method the Lord used to reveal to me a plot of the rich and a warning for the Lord's people.

There is another great benefit from devotional study – learning how to discern the voice of the Lord. When God brings revelation to you from His Word you will know it! You do not have to force the thought or make it up. The thoughts will just come to you as a steady stream and the Holy Spirit will reveal things you did not know or were not even thinking about.

As always, when you receive revelation, I recommend that you check your revelations for confirmation.

Through Bible study (among other ways), the Holy Spirit can reveal anything, anytime, for anyone. For many believers, the Holy Spirit will reveal things that apply to you and your life. However, He may give you a revelation for nations or other people groups. For example, when I receive a revelation, it may also apply to my congregation. When someone such as Bishop Dr. Bill Hamon receives a revelation, it may apply to the entire Christian International Ministries Network (CIMN) or other nations - because that is the level of his responsibility.[59] Some people receive warnings about national disasters, wars, or other things. Whenever the Holy Spirit decides to reveal something, He usually will reveal it to more than one person, and often to someone who has a position or platform that can do something about it. There will also be a witness of the Spirit among those that hear it.

**"Let two or three prophets speak, and let the others judge." (1 Corinthians 14:29)**

But, for most people, the Holy Spirit will reveal things that apply to them or their life.

## Conclusion

Revelation can occur from any method of the Bible studies I have discussed - topical, book, chapter, character, and devotional. I encourage you to mix and match these types to determine which is best for you. Remember to adapt these methods to fit your need and time constraints. The important thing is to get started and be consistent with it daily. I recommend keeping a journal or notebook and writing down all of your revelations.

This is one of the primary reasons for Bible study – to understand God's Word. From revealed knowledge of His Word flows miracles, healings, and breakthrough. Direct revelation from the Word, when acted upon in faith, releases the power of God because His grace and power is upon what He reveals. When God gives you a revelation, act on it in faith and watch the grace and power of God begin to operate. This is why Bible study is so dry to a lot of people. They do not stay with it long enough to receive revealed knowledge and then believe and act upon it. The will of God and His power flow from prayer, Bible study, and a close intimate relationship with the Lord. I believe this is why we as a Body of Christ lack power - there is not enough intimacy with the Lord Jesus Christ.

# Part VII: Advanced Bible Study

Advanced Bible study is for those who want to do advanced research into the Word of God. The word "advanced" does not mean complicated. Rather, in some ways, it is actually easier because of the study tools that are available. Advanced does not mean it is only for theologians or ministry professionals. For the purposes of this discussion, the definition of 'advanced' simply means a higher stage of development or progress.[60] In other words, these types of Bible studies are not for beginners. If you are new to Bible study, I recommend that you become familiar with topical, book, chapter, character or devotional studies so that you will have the skills to do an effective advanced study.

For the purposes of this book, I will address three types of advanced Bible study: word study, computer based, and correspondence courses.

## Word Study

Just as the name implies, word study is a study of the individual words in a scripture. The Old Testament was written in Hebrew and the New Testament was written in Greek. Although most people cannot speak or read these ancient languages, there is a method that people can use to study individual words of the ancient languages. The use of a concordance is one such method. For example, Strong's Exhaustive Concordance of the Bible assigns a number called a 'Strong' number to each word in the King James Version of the Bible. The King James Version was used because it was the only version available in 1890 when this concordance was first published. There are also other concordances available, as well as computer programs that have concordance features. Regardless of your preferred tool, the following is my recommendation for conducting a word study using Strong's Concordance.

1. Look up the word you are studying in the concordance. For example, suppose you are studying the word 'grace.'

**"...To the praise of the glory of his grace, wherein he hath made us accepted in the beloved." (Ephesians 1:6, KJV)**

Look up the English word 'grace' in the Greek dictionary – which is a part of Strong's Concordance. Remember that New Testament words were written in Greek, so this is the reason for checking the Greek dictionary. The dictionary is a part of this reference work, consequently, everything you need to do the word study is in this reference work. In the Greek dictionary we discover that the word 'grace' has been assigned the number 5485.

2. Look up 5485 in Strong's Concordance and you will find the Greek definition of the word 'grace.' Also included is the word written in Konia Greek and the English pronouncement of the word. Greek definitions of words reveal the richness of the language that sometimes is not revealed in English translations. The Greek definition often emphasizes the true meaning of the word.

## Computer Based

Another method to conduct an advanced Bible study is using computer based Bible study programs. Computer programs may save hours of time researching through small print concordances, commentaries, and dictionaries. They vastly speed up the process of study and they are easy to use. Computer programs also contain cultural, historical, and geographical information that may enrich the entire study process.

One recommended computer program is PC Bible Study. This program is available in several different versions, depending on your level of skill with computers and the type of study resources you want in the program. It is easy to use and allows you the benefit of being able to cut and paste research information directly into your outline or paper.

It is worthy to note that there are also free computer Bible study programs that are accessible online. While they may not have the same amount of information, they do get the job done for most study needs. I am personally aware of studylight.org, esword.org and biblegateway.org. It may be helpful for you to try one of these free programs before deciding to invest in a more elaborate program.

One word of caution: Bible study is not just a matter of processing data. It is all too easy to fall into the trap of letting the Bible program become just a resource for messages and outlines.

Remember, the Bible is a living book. It is the inspired Word of God. Nothing should take the place of your quiet time with the Lord and His Word. Flowing in the anointing with a Spirit of Excellence in ministry comes from relationship and not a computer! Computers are good for learning, but what we learn has to be applied to our lives by the Holy Spirit. Learning is one thing, revelation is another. In the passage about the Apostle Peter and the miraculous catch of fish, remember that Peter had information, but Jesus had revelation! (Read Luke 5:4-11). Revelation is what we truly need to answer our problems. This requires going before the Lord in worship and letting the Word speak to us. We should not just read the Bible, but let the Bible read us!

## Correspondence Courses

Another advanced method of Bible study is correspondence courses. The advantage of this method is that the study program is already structured for you. One great way to start this method is to begin with an Old and New Testament Survey course. This type of course will give you a good overview of the entire Bible. It will also help you maintain focus with the added benefit of having someone review and correct your work. Correspondence courses can be done on-line or through the mail. The majority of correspondence schools also assign an instructor to you that can answer your questions as you study. Many of them issue a certificate of completion for each course finished. If you stay consistent with a program like this, your knowledge of the Bible and doctrine will grow immensely. You will understand spiritual truths and have a comprehension of the Bible that you would otherwise not know.

However, there are two important concerns regarding correspondence courses to remember: accreditation and doctrine.

1. ACCREDITATION:

For accreditation, ensure that your courses are fully accredited by ensuring they will transfer to other schools. If you want college credit and are working towards an accredited diploma, I recommend that you check the transfer of credit policy.

A college level correspondence course may involve taking exams through a proctor who is someone who will oversee your testing. This is usually your pastor or spiritual leader.

The process for taking the exam may be strict for correspondence courses. The correspondence school sends your exam to the proctor when you indicate that you are ready for the test. You then make arrangements with your proctor to take the exam. The proctor gives you the exam and observes you during the test to ensure that you are not using your textbook or any other study aid. Generally, most correspondence schools allow you to have your Bible during the exam. The proctor monitors the time limit for the test. When you are finished or time is up, your proctor will collect the exam and mail it to the correspondence school. Because of this strict process and the time it takes to do correspondence courses, I recommend that you begin with a non-accredited course. This will allow you an opportunity to ensure you have the desire for this type of course work.

2. DOCTRINE:

The second concern regarding correspondence courses is doctrine. I recommend that you check the doctrinal background of the school to ensure you agree, before your take the course. For example, if you are a Christian there is no value in taking a course from a school that has non-Christian beliefs or doctrine. If you are interested in understanding the difference between non-Christian beliefs and Biblical Christianity, there are materials on-line or in Christian bookstores that explain it. Another doctrinal concern regards the issue of the Trinity. Some faith based groups do not believe in the Trinity of the God-head, i.e., the Father, Son and Holy Ghost. They consider that Jesus is the only name of God and the only person in the God-head. Consequently, if you believe in the doctrine of the Trinity, then this is another area that warrants your regard. While some may believe that the doctrine of the Trinity is not important, I believe that anything that changes the fundamental revelation and nature of the God-head is very serious. For example, did Jesus think that faith in the Father was important? You be the judge. See His response in John 12:44.

**"Then Jesus cried out and said, He who believes in Me, believes not in Me but in Him who sent Me. And he who sees Me sees Him who sent Me. I have come as a light into the world, that whoever believes in Me should not abide in darkness." (John 12:44)**

**"Whoever denies the Son does not have the Father either; he who acknowledges the Son has the Father also." (1 John 2:23)**

Is there a Trinity of Father, Son, and Holy Spirit? Again you judge. By the mouth of two or three witnesses let every word be established.

**"And Jesus came and spoke to them, saying, "All authority has been given to Me in heaven and on earth. Go therefore and make disciples of all the nations, baptizing them in the name of the Father and of the Son and of the Holy Spirit, teaching them to observe all things that I have commanded you; and lo, I am with you always, even to the end of the age." Amen." (Matthew 28:18-20)**

**"The grace of the Lord Jesus Christ, and the love of God, and the communion of the Holy Spirit be with you all. Amen." (2 Corinthians 13:14)**

Another doctrinal issue regards the doctrine of 'salvation by grace.' For example, some groups hold to doctrines that say you must not do anything on the Sabbath; some apply food restrictions; and some believe in soul sleep. Others maintain a different perspective of end-time events and events that occur after death, such as soul annihilation. Some proclaim that salvation occurs by grace through faith, yet they believe they are saved through righteous works.

But, the Bible declares that it is only through the shed blood of Jesus Christ that we are saved. It is not through works.

When we sin, grace is exactly what we need. Grace provides the power to overcome through faith in what Christ did at the cross. This is the only sacrifice that the Holy Spirit will accept and He makes His power available to those who believe in Jesus Christ as Lord and Savior.

Consequently, I recommend that before you sign up for a correspondence course (or any other Bible course from a school) that you read the schools statement of faith and doctrinal perspectives before taking courses. Also, research the background of the course authors. Finally, I urge you to consult with your pastor or spiritual leader before starting any correspondence course to ensure it is doctrinally correct.

# Conclusion

This book was written with the purpose of making Bible study more meaningful, spiritually refreshing and life giving. The Word of God is alive with life changing power. When studied on a consistent basis, the Word of God will renew your mind and transform you into the image of Christ.

This book has seven parts:
Part I: What is the Bible
Part II: Purpose of the Bible
Part III: Why & How Study the Bible
Part IV: How Did We Obtain the Bible
Part V: Interpretation of the Bible
Part VI: Study Methods & Types
Part VII: Advanced Bible Study

In Part I we learned that the Bible is divided into 66 sections that are called 'books,' 39 books are in the Old Testament and 27 books are in the New Testament. Twenty-two of these books are historical, five are poetical, 18 are prophetic, and 21 are written in letter form. The scriptures contain revelation, poetry, songs, hymns, history, biography, stories, parables, law, and most importantly – they reveal God's nature. The Bible was written as men were inspired by the Holy Spirit. This inspiration guarantees that the Bible is infallible and inerrant in every way.

In Part II we addressed seven purposes of the Bible: 1) to reveal the person of Jesus Christ as the Savior of the world; 2) to reveal the purpose for creation and plan of redemption for mankind; 3) to reveal God's character, His standard of holiness, and great love for us; 4) to reveal God's principles; 5) the Word of God is the source of faith and hope; 6) to reveal things to come and that evil will not prevail; 7) Seventh, the Bible discloses what happens to us after we die and where we will be eternally. It tells us that there is a heaven and a hell.

In Part III we learned why and how to study the Bible. We need to study the Bible to learn about Jesus and have a better relationship with Him. Reading the Word will transform us into His image and will give us courage to face our realities, knowledge to overcome, comfort for our mourning, and instruction to live in a Godly manner.

In Part IV we learned what the Bible is and how we obtained it. The Bible is the inspired, infallible, and inerrant Word of God. The scriptures reveal God's plan for man and plan of salvation. There are at least 36 different authors who wrote from different continents, countries, languages, occupations touching all the experiences of mankind - extending over 1,500 years. And yet the Bible is one cohesive book because God was the real author! We learned that we obtained the Bible from manuscripts made of various materials such as papyrus and animal skins. We also addressed how the copies were carefully produced, maintained, and translated.

In Part V we discussed how to interpret the Bible. I suggested that the interpretation of scripture should be more accurate as you apply the general guidelines of context, receive, meditate, interpret, and apply. However, if you are still having difficulty, ask your pastor, check a commentary, or ask the Holy Spirit to reveal it to you.

In Part VI we discussed study methods and types of Bible study. Revelation can occur from any method of the Bible studies we discussed - topical, book, chapter, character, and devotional. The important thing is to get started and be consistent with it daily. I recommend keeping a journal or notebook and writing down all of your revelations. Miracles, healing, and breakthrough in life flow from believing on God's Word; and study will cause your faith to grow. Direct revelation from the Word, when acted upon in faith, releases the power of God. When God gives you a revelation, act on it in faith and watch the grace and power of God begin to operate.

In Part VII we discussed advanced Bible study for those who want to do advanced research into the Word of God. For the purposes of this book, we addressed three types: word study, computer based, and correspondence courses.

It is my hope that this book will enrich your spirit and renew your mind so that you will have a greater love for Jesus and a greater understanding of His Word. I leave you with this one last thought - perhaps it is the one you should study first?

**"So then faith comes by hearing, and hearing by the word of God." (Romans 10:17)**

# Prayers

## "Rejoice always, pray without ceasing, in everything give thanks; for this is the will of God in Christ Jesus for you." (1 Thessalonians 5:16-18)

The Bible exhorts us to always pray. Prayer is the furnace in any individual. Below are some recommended prayers for use during your personal devotions.

### Prayer for Salvation:

Lord, I ask you to come into my heart and forgive me of my sins. I want to live for you. In Jesus Name, Amen.

### Prayer for Revelation:

Lord, I ask you to give me the spirit of wisdom and revelation in the knowledge of you. Open my eyes that I may see and understand your Word. Help me to understand what my calling in life is and what is the exceeding greatness of your power. In Jesus Name, Amen. (Based on Ephesians 1:17-21)

### Prayer for Faith and Trust in God:

Lord, increase my faith in you and cause me to be mindful of your grace in my life. Cause me to trust in your unfailing love and mercy. I thank you for redeeming me from all circumstances in my life and for surrounding me with your loving kindness. Cause me not to fear, but to always look to you, the Author and the Finisher of my faith. In Jesus Name, Amen.

## Prayer for a Vision and Destiny:

Lord, thank you for pouring the fresh oil of your anointing into my life. Reveal your Word to me and give me a new vision for the future that will be your perfect will and timing for my life. Let me always come into agreement with your perfect will for my life and bring me into the prophetic destiny you have ordained for my life. In Jesus Name, Amen.

## Prayer of Thanksgiving:

Lord, thank you for being my savior, redeemer, healer, high tower, deliverer, and shield. Thank you for protecting me from all enemies. Thank you for being the guiding light of this nation and my life. Thank you for causing me to be blessed in our jobs, in our homes, and for giving us health, prosperity, and the desires of our heart. Thank you for causing all grace to abound toward us that we have sufficiency in all things. Most of all, I thank you for your love toward me that surpasses all understanding and can never fail. In Jesus Name, Amen.

## Prayer for Healing:

Lord, I ask you to heal my heart, mind and soul from memories of the past, and to bring healing to my physical body. I ask your healing anointing to flow through me to completely restore me. In Jesus Name, Amen.

## Prayer for the Family:

Lord, thank you for blessing me with my family and I ask you to save them from sin. Bring them to repentance and reveal yourself to them. In Jesus Name, Amen.

# Charge

**The charge of every believer is to "Go therefore and make disciples of all the nations, baptizing them in the name of the Father and of the Son and of the Holy Spirit, teaching them to observe all things that I have commanded you; and lo, I am with you always, even to the end of the age." (Matthew 28:19)**

We charge you in the name of the Lord Jesus Christ to go forth in the power and anointing of the Holy Spirit, to be used by Him for the furtherance of His Kingdom, and to receive greater knowledge and revelation of Him and His Word.

---

*To order books or for ministry engagements contact:*

Covenant Life Church
P.O. Box 1262
Springfield, VA 22151
703-280-0341
www.covenant-life-church.org
www.propheticlifeministries.org

# Endnotes

[1]Dynamics. (n.d.). Retrieved March 9, 2014, from http://www.merriam-webster.com/dictionary/dynamics
[2]Author's definition.
[3]Inspiration. (1995). Strong's exhaustive concordance: New American standard Bible. (Updated Ed.). Retrieved from http://www.biblestudytools.com/concordances/strongs-exhaustive-concordance
[4]Author's definition.
[5]Infallible. (n.d.). Retrieved March 9, 2014, from http://www.merriam-webster.com/dictionary/infallible
[6]Mullins, Mary. Galway, Ireland. Retrieved 5 March 2014, from http://www.moytura.com/reflections/busy.htm
[7]Crowley, Rory P. (2011). Athens 2011: Four new Manuscript Discoveries on My First Trip Abroad. Retrieved March 5, 2014 from http://www.csntm.org/Blog/Archive/2011/6/2/Athens2011
[8]Dunn, Jimmy. (2014). Historical Papyrus. Retrieved March 3, 2014 from http://www.touregypt.net/featurestories/papyrus.htm retrieved
[9]Ibid
[10]Ibid
[11]Parchment. (n.d.). *Dictionary.com Unabridged*. Retrieved March 09, 2014, from Dictionary.com website: http://dictionary.reference.com/browse/parchment
[12] Orr, James, M.A., D.D. General Editor. "Definition for 'PARCHMENTS'". "International Standard Bible Encyclopedia". Retrieved on March 9, 2014 from http://www.bible-history.com/isbe/P/PARCHMENTS/
[13]Orr, James, M.A., D.D. General Editor. "Definition for 'PARCHMENTS'". "International Standard Bible Encyclopedia". Retrieved on March 9, 2014 from http://www.bible-history.com/isbe/W/WRITING%2C+2/

---

[14]Ibid.
[15]Orr, James, M.A., D.D. General Editor. "Entry for 'SCRIBES'". "International Standard Bible Encyclopedia". 1915. Retrieved on March 9, 2014 from http://www.biblestudytools.com/dictionary/scribes/
[16]Ibid.
[17]The Dead Sea scroll library. Israel antiquities authority. Qumran caves Scrolls. Retrieved March 9, 2014 from http://www.deadseascrolls.org.il/learn-about-the-scrolls/introduction
[18]Scribes. Retrieved March 3, 2014 from http://www.biblestudytools.com/dictionary/scribes/
[19]Dead Sea Scrolls. Retrieved March 3, 2014 from http://www.deadseascrolls.org.il/learn-about-the-scrolls/introduction
[20]The Dead Sea scroll library. Israel antiquities authority. Qumran caves Scrolls. Retrieved March 9, 2014 from http://www.deadseascrolls.org.il/learn-about-the-scrolls/introduction
[21]Author's definition.
[22]Faith Facts, Gospel Communications Network. (2008). Article, "How do you know that the Bible is true? Isn't it just a bunch of fables?" Retrieved March 2, 2014 from http://www.faithfacts.org/search-for-truth/questions-of-christians/how-do-you-know-that-the-bible-is-true
[23]Scribes. Retrieved March 3, 2014 from http://www.biblestudytools.com/dictionary/scribes/
[24]Dead Sea Scrolls. Retrieved March 3, 2014 from http://www.deadseascrolls.org.il/learn-about-the-scrolls/introduction
[25]Hittites. Encyclopaedia Judaica, the Gale Group (2008). Retrieved March 9, 2014 from http://www.jewishvirtuallibrary.org/jsource/judaica/ejud_0002_0009_0_09061.html.

[26]Easton, Matthew George. "Entry for Canon". "Easton's Bible Dictionary". Retrieved March 9, 2014 from http://www.biblestudytools.com/dictionary/canon/
[27]Ibid.
[28]Ibid.
[29]Ibid.
[30]Author's definition.
[31]Thomas Nelson, New Kings Version Bible. Preface.
[32]Jerome, Saint. The Columbia Encyclopedia, 6th ed. 2013. Retrieved March 05, 2014 from Encyclopedia.com: http://www.encyclopedia.com/doc/1E1-Jerome-S.html
33Ibid.
[34]Vulgate. (n.d.). Collins English Dictionary - Complete & Unabridged 10th Edition. Retrieved March 05, 2014, from Dictionary.com website: http://dictionary.reference.com/browse/vulgate
[35]Tyndale, William. The Columbia Encyclopedia, 6th ed. 2013. Retrieved March 05, 2014 from Encyclopedia.com: http://www.encyclopedia.com/topic/William_Tyndale.aspx#2-1E1:Tyndale-full
[36]Ibid.
[37]The Crown Copyright, The official website of the British Monarchy, Henry VIII. Retrieved March 9, 2014 from https://www.royal.gov.uk/HistoryoftheMonarchy/KingsandQueensofEngland/TheTudors/HenryVIII.aspx.
[38]Ibid.
[39]The Crown Copyright, The official website of the British Monarchy, James I. Retrieved March 9, 2014 from https://www.royal.gov.uk/HistoryoftheMonarchy/KingsandQueensoftheUnitedKingdom/TheStuarts/JamesI.aspx
[40]Author's definition.

[41]Author's definition.
[42]Begotten. (n.d.). Dictionary.com Unabridged. Retrieved March 09, 2014, from http://dictionary.reference.com/browse/parchment
[43]Monogeneses. Retrieved March 9, 2014 from http://dictionary.reference.com/browse/monogeneses
[44]Tongues. (1995). In Strong's exhaustive concordance: New American standard Bible. (Updated ed.). Retrieved from http://www.biblestudytools.com/concordances/strongs-exhaustive-concordance/tongues
[45]Author's definition.
[46]Allegorical. (n.d.). Retrieved March 9, 2014, from http://www.merriam-webster.com/dictionary/allegorical
[47]Author's definition.
[48]Easton, Matthew George. "Entry for Parable". "Easton's Bible Dictionary". Retrieved March 9, 2014 from http://www.biblestudytools.com/dictionary/parable/
[49]Author's definition.
[50]Author's definition.
[51]Author's definition
[52]Author's definition.
[53]Author's definition.
[54]Devotion. (1995). In Strong's exhaustive concordance: New American standard Bible. (Updated ed). OT Strong's reference number 2612.
[55]Devotion. (1995). In Strong's exhaustive concordance: New American standard Bible. (Updated ed). NT Strong's reference number 4574.
[56]Devotion. (n.d.). Retrieved March 9, 2014, from http://www.merriam-webster.com/dictionary/devotion
[57]Italicized words are inserted by the author.
[58]Italicized words are inserted by the author.

---

[59]Hamon, Bill., Dr. Bishop, Christian International Network of Minsters (CIMN). http://christianinternational.com/
[60]Author's definition.

Made in USA - North Chelmsford, MA
1311744_9780972318525
04.18.2022 1519